Pratyabhijñāhṛdayam

BY THE SAME AUTHOR

*

THE CONCEPTION OF BUDDHIST NIRVANA

*

AN INTRODUCTION TO MADHYAMAKA PHILOSOPHY

*

SIVA-SUTRAS: THE YOGA OF SUPREME IDENTITY

*

SPANDA-KARIKAS: THE DIVINE CREATIVE PULSATION

*

PARATRISIKA-VIVARANA BY ABHINAVAGUPTA

*

VIJNANABHAIRAVA OR DIVINE CONSCIOUSNESS

Pratyabhijñāhṛdayam

The Secret of Self-Recognition

Sanskrit Text with English Translation Notes and Introduction

Jaideva Singh

MOTILAL BANARSIDASS
INTERNATIONAL
DELHI

Reprint Edition : Delhi, 2021, 2023
First Edition : Delhi, 1963

ISBN : 978-93-92510-07-6 (Cloth)
ISBN : 978-93-92510-08-3 (Paper)

Also available at

MOTILAL BANARSIDASS INTERNATIONAL

H. O. : 41 U.A. Bungalow Road, (Back Lane) Jawahar Nagar, Delhi - 110 007
4261/3 (basement), Ansari Road, Darya Ganj, New Delhi - 110 002
203 Royapettah High Road, Mylapore, Chennai - 600 004
12/1A, 2nd Floor, Bankim Chatterjee Street, Kolkata - 700 073
Stockist : Motilal Books, Ashok Rajpath, Near Kali Mandir, Patna - 800 004

Printed & Bound by
MOTILAL BANARSIDASS INTERNATIONAL

Dedicated With Profound
Respects to
SWĀMĪ LAKṢMAṆA JOO
To Whom Alone I Owe
Whatever Little I Know of
Pratyabhijñā Philosophy

PREFACE TO THE FOURTH EDITION

In this edition misprints occurring in the previous edition have been corrected.

Alteration in the text of the translation has been made at a few places for the sake of greater clarity.

The notes have been improved upon at a few places.

Varanasi
1982

JAIDEVA SINGH

PREFACE TO THE SECOND EDITION

In this edition, both the Introduction and Notes have been considerably enlarged.

In the Introduction, three new topics, viz., Svātantryavāda and Ābhāsavāda, Ṣaḍadhvā and Comparison and Contrast with Śaṁkara's Advaitavāda have been added. Considerable new additions have been made in the Notes.

At some places, alteration has been made in the translation of the text for the sake of greater clarity.

With these additions and alterations, the book has been greatly improved and will, it is hoped, be of considerable value to the readers.

VARANASI
1977

JAIDEVA SINGH

PREFACE TO THE THIRD EDITION

In this edition, a few misprints that had crept in have been corrected.

Alteration in the translation of the text has been made at two or three places for the sake of greater clarity.

The whole book has been thoroughly revised.

Varanasi
1980

JAIDEVA SINGH

PREFACE TO THE FIRST EDITION

Pratyabhjiñāhṛdayam serves as the best introduction to the Pratyabhijñā philosophy of Kashmir. An English translation of the book by Prof. K.F. Leidecker is already available. My only apology for bringing out another translation of the book is that the one that is available bristles with mistakes, some of which are quite serious. It has been my painful duty to point out a few of the serious mistakes. No one who has not studied this book with a teacher can work away its translation merely with the assistance of a lexicon and grammar. I had the good fortune of studying it with Swami Lakshman Joo who is practically the sole surviving exponent of this system in Kashmir, and who not only embodies within himself the tradition of the school, but has also practised the *yogic* disciplines recommended by it. He has helped me not only by explaining the technical words but also in tracing out the sources of most of the quotations occurring in the book. I am deeply grateful to him for his kind help.

The Sanskrit text adopted is that of the Kashmir Sanskrit Series. The translation is given below each page of the text. It closely follows the original—with a few words here and there in parenthesis to make the sense clearer. A person knowing even a little of Sanskrit can follow the translation almost word for word. I have tried to make the translation as flawless as possible. Some of the highly technical terms have been used in it as they occur in the original, but their connotation has been elaborately elucidated in the notes.

An introduction containing the chief features of the Pratyabhijñā system has been provided. An analysis of the contents of each *Sūtra* has also been given. Copious notes on difficult and technical words have been added, and a glossary of the technical terms has also been appended at the end.

While the book was at the proof stage, I referred my difficulties in some of the *Sūtras* to MM. Dr. Gopinath Kaviraja and profited greatly by his illuminating exposition. I have used his suggestions with advantage in some of my notes. I am deeply grateful to him for his kind help. Acharya Pandit Rameshwar Jha was helpful in the clarification of some difficult passages of the text. I, therefore, offer him my heart-felt thanks.

JAIDEVA SINGH

CONTENTS

INTRODUCTION

Preliminary

The Śaiva religion is perhaps the most ancient faith of the world. Sir John Marshall says in his *Mohenjodaro and the Indus Civilization* that excavations in Mohenjodaro and Harappa reveal an important fact, viz., that Śivaism has a history going back to the Chalcolithic Age or even further still, and that it thus takes its place as the most ancient living faith in the world. It had many off-shoots and appeared in different forms in many parts of the world. In India, there are three main forms of this religio-philosophy, viz., the Vīra-Śaiva form in Deccan-Karṇāṭaka, the Śaiva-siddhānta in Tamila Nāḍu, and the Advaita Śaiva form in Kashmir. There are some common features in all the three, but there are important differences also. Here we are concerned with the Advaita Śaiva Philosophy of Kashmir.

In India, there is no such thing as arm-chair philosophy. Philosophy is not only a way of thought, but also a way of life in this country. It is not born of idle curiosity, nor is it a mere intellectual game. Every philosophy here is a religion, and every religion has its philosophy. The philosopher here was not a tall and spectacled professor dictating his notes to the class or weaving cob-webs of theory in his study, but one who was moved by a deep inner urge to know the secrets of life, who lived laborious days of spiritual discipline and who saw the light by the transformation of his life. Moved by pity for his fellow-men, he tried to interpret the truth he had experienced to the logical reason of man. Thus arose philosophy in this country.

The Advaita Śaiva Philosophy of Kashmir was of this type. For centuries, it was imparted as a secret doctrine to the aspirant who had to live it and test it in the laboratory of the Self. In course of time only the cult and the ritual remained; the philosophical background was forgotten. Perhaps, a select few still knew the philosophical doctrine by oral tradition, but the first thinker known to history, who reduced the main principles to writing was, Vasugupta. He is said to have lived towards the end of the eighth or the beginning of the ninth century A.D. Since then, philosophical writing had been an active and continued process in Kashmir which went on for nearly four centuries. The literature on this system has accumulated to such an extent that it would require almost a life-time to study it. Some works of the system have still not been published.

Śaiva Literature

The literature of the Śaiva or Trika system may be broadly divided into three : (a) *Āgama Śāstra*, (b) *Spanda Śāstra*, (c) *Pratyabhijñā Śāstra*.

(a) *Āgama Śāstra*

This is believed to be a revelation and has been handed down from teacher to pupil. Some of the works under this heading are :

Mālinivijaya, *Svacchanda*, *Vijñānabhairava*, *Mṛgendra*, *Rudra-yāmala*, *Śiva-Sūtras*. On the *Śiva-Sūtras* there are the Vṛtti, the Vārttika of Bhāskara and Varadarāja and the Vimarśinī commentary by Kṣemarāja. There are commentaries on some of the *tantras* also.

(b) *Spanda Śāstra*

This lays down the important doctrines of the system. The main works under this heading are :

The *Spanda Sūtras* or the *Spanda Kārikās*. These elaborate the principles of the Śiva-Sūtras. On these, there are the following commentaries :

Vivṛti by Rāmakaṇṭha, *Pradīpikā* by Utpala Vaiṣṇava, *Spandasandoha* by Kṣemarāja, and *Spandanirṇaya* by Kṣemarāja. *Spandasandoha* contains a commentary only on the first Kārikā.

(c) *Pratyabhijñā Śāstra*

This contains arguments and counter-arguments, discussions, and reasonings. This interprets the main doctrines of the system to the logical reason of man.

Somānanda composed *Śivadṛṣṭi*. Another important work is *Īśvarapratyabhijñā* by Utpala, pupil of Somānanda. There are the following commentaries on this :

Vṛtti by the author himself, *Pratyabhijñāvimarśinī* and *Pratyabhijñā-vivṛti-vimarśini* by Abhinavagupta.

A digest of the Pratyabhijñā Śāstra, named *Pratyabhijñāhṛdayam* was prepared by Kṣemarāja.

Abhinavagupta's *Tantrāloka* in 12 Volumes and his *Tantrālokasāra* give an exhaustive treatment of all the important doctrines and disciplines of the system.[1]

Pratyabhijñāhṛdayam

As said above, this is a digest of the Pratyabhijñā system prepared by Kṣemaraja. He was the brilliant pupil of Abhinavagupta, a versatile genius who was a peerless master of tantra, yoga, philosophy, poetics, and dramaturgy. According to Dr. K.C. Pandey, Abhinavagupta flourished in the tenth century A.D. Since Kṣemarāja was his pupil, he must have also lived in the tenth century. He wrote the following works :

Pratyabhijñāhṛdayam, *Spandasandoha*, *Spandanirṇaya*, *Svacchandodyota*, *Netrodyota*, *Vijñānadhairavodyota*, *Sivasūtra-vimarśinī*, *Stavacintāmaṇiṭikā*, *Parāprāveśikā*, *Tattvasandoha*.

Very little is known of the life and parentage of Kṣemarāja. It has been very rightly said that his book, *Pratyabhijñāhṛdayam* occupies the same place in Śaiva or Trika literature as Vedāntasāra does in Vedānta. It avoids all polemics and gives in a very succinct form the main tenets of the Pratyabhijñā system. He says at the very outset of his work :

इह ये सुकुमारमतयोऽकृततीक्ष्णतर्कशास्त्रपरिश्रमाः शक्तिपातोन्मिषितपारमेश्वरसमावेशाभिलाषिणः कतिचित् भक्तिभाजः तेषामीश्वरप्रत्यभिज्ञोपदेशतत्त्वं मनाक् उन्मील्यते ।

1. I am indebted to J.C. Chatterji's *Kashmir Shaivism* for the historical account given above.

"In this world, there are some devoted people who are undeveloped in reflection and have not taken pains in studying difficult works (like Logic and Dialectics), but who nevertheless aspire after *Samāveśa* with the Highest Lord which blossoms forth with the descent of Śakti. For their sake the truth of the teachings of Īśvarapratyabhijñā is being explained briefly."

He regarded *Īśvarabratyabhijñā* of Utpalācārya as a very great work on this system, and has provided a ready and easy manual for those who are inclined as a result of Divine grace to know the main principles of 'pratyabhijñā', but are unable to study the great work of Utpalācārya, because of their lack of training in Logic and Dialectics. He has succeeded remarkably well in condensing in a short compass all the important principles of Īśvarapratyabhijñā and has avoided its rigoristic logical discussion. The book is, therefore, of supreme importance for those who want to have an elementary knowledge of 'pratyabhijñā'. He has composed the Sūtras as well as written the commentary.

The word 'pratyabhijñā' means re-cognition. The individual Self or *jīva* is divine or Śiva, but he has forgotten his real nature, and is identified with his psycho-physical mechanism. The teaching is meant to enable him to recognise his real nature, to bring home to him the truth that his real Self is none other than Śiva and to suggest to him the spiritual discipline by which he can attain 'at-one-ment' with Him.

The details of the teaching will be found in the body of the book. Here we may review the main ideas of the system under the following heads :

1. Ultimate Reality 2. The Universe or the World Process. 3. Svātantryavāda and Ābhāsavāda 4. Ṣaḍadhvā 5. Comparison and Contrast with Śaṁkara's Advaitavāda 6. The Individual Self 7. Bondage 8. Liberation.

1. *Ultimate Reality*

Reality in its ultimate aspect is Cit or Parāsaṁvit. *Cit* or Parāsaṁvit is untranslatable in any other language. Generally it is translated 'consciousness'. I have myself done so for want of a better word. But it should be clearly understood that *Cit* is not exactly consciousness. The word *Con*-sciousness connotes subject-object relation, knower-known duality. But *Cit* is not relational. It is just the *changeless principle* of all changing experience. It is Parāsaṁvit. It has, so to speak, the *immediacy* of feeling where neither the 'I', nor the 'This' is distinguished. It is the 'coalescence into undivided unity' of 'I' and 'This'. Perhaps, the word 'sciousness' may, to some extent, express the idea contained in Cit or Parāsaṁvit. To use the verb contained in consciousness, the Ultimate Reality or Supreme Self is the Self *Sciring Itself*. In the words of Pratyabhijñā Śāstra, it is, *prakāśavimarśamaya*. The Supreme Self is called Parama Śiva. This is not only *prakāśa*. The word 'prakāśa' again is untranslatable. Literally, it means light, illumination. Just as light makes every thing visible, even so that being there, every thing else is. In the words of Kaṭhopaniṣad—'*Tameva bhāntam anubhāti sarvam, tasya bhāsā sarvamidam vibhāti*'. 'It shining, every thing happens to shine. By its light alone does all this appear.' Śāṅkara Vedānta also calls Ultimate Reality 'prakāśa', but the sun is 'prakāśa; even a diamond is 'prakāśa'. What is the difference between the two ? The Śaiva philosophy says, "Ultimate Reality is not simply *prakāśa* : it is also *vimarśa*". What is this *vimarśa* ? This word again is untranslatable. Perhaps the word 'Sciring' may help. Ultimate Reality is not only Sciousness (prakāśa), but a Sciousness that also *scires* itself (vimarśa). It is not simply *prakāśa* lying inert like a diamond, but *surveys* itself. This Sciring or Surveying of itself by Ultimate Reality is called *Vimarśa*. As Kṣemarāja has put it in his *Parāprāveśikā* (p.2) it is "akṛtrimāham iti visphuraṇam"; it is the *non-relational*, *immediate* awareness of I. What this 'akṛtrima-aham' is, we shall see later on. If Ultimate Reality were merely *prakāśa* and not also *vimarśa*, it would be powerless and inert. "*Yadi nirvimarśaḥ syāt anīśvaro jaḍaśca prasajyeta*" (*Parāprāveśikā*, p. 2) It is this pure I-consciousness or *Vimarśa* that is responsible for the manifestation, maintenance and reabsorption of the universe.

Cit *scires* itself as *Cidrūpiṇī Śakti*. This sciring itself as *Cidrūpiṇī Śakti* is *Vimarśa*. Therefore, *vimarśa* has been named differently as *parāśakti, parāvāk, Svātantrya, aiśvarya, kartṛtva, sphurattā, Sāra, hṛdaya, Spanda.* (See *Parāprāveśika* p. 2)

It will thus be seen that the Ultimate Reality is not only Universal Consciousness but also Universal Psychic Energy or Power. This All-inclusive Universal Consciousness is also called Anuttara i.e., the Reality than which there is nothing that may be called higher—the Highest Reality, the Absolute. It is both transcendental (*viśvottīrna*) and immanent (*viśvmaya*).

The Śaiva philosophy has been called Realistic Idealism by some writers. I do not think this is a happy characterization of the Śaiva philosophy. The approach of the Idealists of the West is entirely different from that of the thinkers of the Śaiva philosophy. To characterize it in terms of the Western Idealists is only to create confusion. The word 'idea' has played havoc in Western philosophy, and it would not be right to import that havoc in Śaiva philosophy. Ultimate Reality is not a mere 'idea' whatever that may mean, but Self underlying all reality, the Changeless Principle of all manifestation.

2. *Manifestation—the Universe—or the World Process*

Whether we call Ultimate Reality Sciousness or Consciousness, it is not something blank. It has infinite powers, and contains in a potential form all that is ever likely to be. It is the *Svabhāva* or nature of Ultimate Reality to manifest. If Ultimate Reality did not manifest, it would no longer be consciousness or Self, but something like an object or not-Self. As Abhinavagupta puts it :

"अस्थास्यदेकरूपेण वपुषा चेन्महेश्वरः ।
महेश्वरत्वं संवित्त्वं तदत्यक्ष्यद् घटादिवत् ॥"

—Tantr. III. 100

"If the Highest Reality did not manifest in infinite variety, but remained cooped up within its solid singleness, it would neither be the Highest Power nor Consciousness, but something like a jar".

We have seen that Ultimate Reality or Parama Śiva is '*prakāśa-vimarśamaya*'. In that state the 'I' and the 'This' are in an undivided unity. The 'I' is the '*prakāśa*' aspect, and the

'This' or Its consciousness of It as itself is the '*vimarśa*' aspect. This *Vimarśa* is *Svātantrya*, Absolute will or *Śakti*. This *Śakti* has been called as 'the Heart of the Supreme Lord' in *Parāprāveśikā* by Kṣemarāja (*hrdayam parameśituḥ*). But *Śakti* is only another aspect of the Supreme Self. In the Supreme experience, the so-called 'This' is nothing but the Self. There is one Self experiencing Itself. This *Vimarśa* or *Śakti* is not contentless. It contains all that is to be.

यथा न्यग्रोधबीजस्थः शक्तिरूपो महाद्रुमः ।
तथा हृदयबीजस्थं विश्वमेतच्चराचरम् ॥

—*Parātrimśikā* 24

"As the great banyan tree lies only in the form of *potency* in the seed, even so the entire universe with all the mobile and immobile beings lies as a potency in the heart of the Supreme".

Another example that is usually given is that of the peacock. Just as a peacock with all its variegated plumage lies as a mere potency in the plasma of its egg, even so the entire universe lies in the *Śakti* of the Supreme. The *Śakti* of the Supreme is called *Citi* or *parā-śakti* or *parā-vāk*.

Parama Śiva has infinite Śakti, but the following five may be considered to be the main ones :

1. *Cit*—the power of Self-revelation by which the Supreme shines by Himself. In this aspect the Supreme is known as Śiva.

2. *Ānanda*—This is absolute bliss. This is also called Svātantrya—absolute Will which is able to do anything without any extraneous aid. (*Svātantryam ānandaśaktiḥ* : *Tantrasāra*-Āhn. 1). In this aspect, the Supreme is known as Śakti. In a sense *Cit* and *ānanda* are the very *svarūpa* (nature) of the Supreme. The rest may be called His Śaktis.

3. *Icchā*—the Will to do this or that, to create. In this aspect, He is known as Sadāśiva or Sādākhya.

4. *Jñāna*—the power of knowing. In this aspect, He is known as Īśvara.

5. *Kriyā*—the power of assuming any and every form (*Sarvākārayogitvam Kriyāśaktiḥ* : *Tantrasāra* Āhn. 1). In this aspect, He is known as *Sadvidyā* or *Śuddha Vidyā*.

The Universe is nothing but an opening out (*unmeṣa*) or expansion (*prasara*) of the Supreme or rather of the Supreme as Śakti.

1. *The Tattvas of the Universal Experience* : 1-5

We have seen that Parama Śiva has two aspects, viz., transcendental (*viśvottirṇa*) and immanent or creative (*viśvamaya*). This creative aspect of Parama Śiva is called *Śiva tattva.*

(1) *Śiva tattva** is the initial creative movement (*prathama spanda*) of Parama Śiva. As has been said in *Ṣaṭtriṁśat-tattva-sandoha* :

यदयमनुत्तरमूर्तिर्निजेच्छयाखिलमिदं जगत्स्रष्टुम ।
पस्पन्दे स स्पन्दः प्रथमः शिवतत्त्वमुच्यते तज्ज्ञैः ॥

—verse 1

When Anuttara or The Absolute by His *Svātantrya* or Absolute Will feels like letting go the Universe contained in Him, the first vibration or throb of this Will is known as Śiva.

(2) *Sakti tattva* is the Energy of Śiva. Śakti in her jñāna aspect is the principle of *negation* (*niṣedha-vyāpāra-rūpā*). ***Śakti, at first, negates*** the 'This' or ***the objective side of experience in Śiva.*** The state in which ***objectivity is negated*** is called the very void. In Cit or Parā Saṁvit, the 'I' and the 'This' are in an indistinguishable unity. In *Śiva tattva*, the 'This' is withdrawn through the operation of *Śakti tattva*, so that the 'I' side of the experience alone remains. This *state* is called *Anāśrita-Śiva* by Kṣemarāja. As he puts it :

श्री परमशिवः ··· पूर्वं चिदैक्याख्यातिमयानाश्रितशिवपर्यायशून्यातिशून्यात्मतया प्रकाशाभेदेन प्रकाशमानतया स्फुरति ।

Śiva in this state appears a mere 'I' devoid of any objective content. In order that Śiva may appear as the Universe, a break in the unitary experience becomes a necessary phase. But this is only a passing phase. To the Subjectivity disengaged from the objective content, the Universe is presented again

*The word 'tattva' is untranslatable, It means the 'thatness' of a thing. The nearest English word is 'principle'.

not as an indistinguishable unity but, an "I-This" in which both are distinguishable but not separable, as they form part of the same Self.

Śakti polarizes Consciousness into *Aham* and *Idam* (I and This)—subject and object.

Śakti, however, is nothing separate from Śiva, but is Śiva Himself in His creative aspect. She is His *Aham-vimarśa* (I-consciousness), His *unmukhatā*—intentness to create. As Maheśvarānanda puts it beautifully in his *Mahārthamañjari* (p. 40, Trivandrum Edition) :

स एव विश्वमेषितुं ज्ञातुं कर्तुं चोन्मुखो भवन् ।
शक्तिस्वभावः कथितो हृदयत्रिकोणमधुमांसलोल्लासः ।।

"He (i.e., Śiva) Himself full of joy enhanced by the honey of the three corners of his heart, viz., Icchā or Will, Jñāna or Knowledge, Kriyā or action, raising up His face to gaze at (His own splendour) is called Śakti".

Maheśvarānanda explains this further in the following words :

यदा स्वहृदयवर्तिनमुक्तरूपमर्थंतत्त्वं बहिःकर्तुंमुन्मुखो भवति तदा शक्तिरिति व्यवह्रियते. (p. 40)

"When He becomes intent to roll out the entire splendour of the Universe that is contained in His heart (in a germinal form), he is designated as Śakti." Śakti is, therefore, his intentness to create.

Śakti is the active or kinetic aspect of Consciousness.

An idea parallel to Vimarśa or unmukhatā is found in the Chāndogyopaniṣad 6. 2. 1-3:

सदेव सौम्य इदमग्र आसीदेकमेवाद्वितीयम्···तदैक्षत, बहु स्याम्. प्रजायेय इति ।

At first (logically, not chronologically) there was only 'Sat' —all alone without a second. He gazed and bethought to Himself "May I be many, may I procreate !"

This *Īkṣitṛtva* or *Īkṣitakarma* is parallel to *Vimarśa* or *unmukhatā* but the implications of this *Īkṣitakarma* have not been developed by Śāṅkara Vedānta.

The Śaiva philosophy does not conceive of the Supreme as a logomachist but as an Artist. Just as an artist cannot contain his delight within himself, but pours it out into a song, a picture or a poem, even so the Supreme Artist pours out the delightful wonder of His splendour into manifestation or creation. Kṣemarāja gives expression to the same idea in his commentary on Utpaladeva's *Stotrāvali* :

आनन्दोच्छलिता शक्तिः सृजत्यात्मानमात्मना ।

"Śakti thrown up by delight lets Herself go forth into manifestation."

All manifestation is, therefore, only a process of experiencing out, creative ideation of Śiva.

In Śakti tattva, *ānanda* aspect of the Supreme is predominant.

Śiva and Śakti *tattvas* can never be disjoined; they remain for ever united whether in creation or dissolution—Śiva as the Experiencing Priniciple, experiencing Himself as pure-'I', and Śakti as profound bliss. Strictly speaking, *Śiva-Śakti tattva* is not an emanation or *ābhāsa*, but the Seed of all emanation.

3. *Sadāśiva or Sādākhya Tattva*

The will (Icchā) to affirm the 'This' side of the 'Universal Experience is known as *Sadāśiva Tattva* or *Sādākhya Tattva.* In Sadāśiva, Icchā or Will is predominant. The experience of this stage is I *am*. Since 'am' or 'being' is affirmed in this stage, it is called *Sādākhya Tattva* ('Sat' meaning 'being') but 'am' implies 'this' (I *am*, but '*am*' what ?—I am 'this'). The experience of this stage is, therefore, 'I am this', but the 'this' is only a hazy experience (*asphuṭa*). The predominant side is still 'I'. The Ideal Universe is experienced as an indistinct something in the depth of consciousness. That is why this experience is called '*nimeṣa*'.

निमेषोऽन्तः सदाशिवः

The 'This' (*Idam*) is faintly experienced by 'I' (*Aham*) as a part of the One Self; the emphasis is however, on the 'I' side of experience. The 'This' (*Idam*) or the universe at this stage is like a hazy idea of the picture that an artist has at the initial stage of his creation. Rājānaka Ānanda in his *Vivaraṇa* on *Ṣaṭtriṁśat-tattvasandoha* very rightly says :

तत्र प्रोन्मीलितमात्रचित्रकल्पतया इदमंशस्य अस्फुटत्वात् इच्छाप्राधान्यम् ।

(p. 3)

"In that stage, the 'This' side of the Experience is hazy like a picture of an artist which is about to be portrayed and hence which is still in an ideal state (i.e., in the state of an idea). Hence in this state it is Will that is predominant." That is why Kṣemarāja says in his *Pratyabhijñāhṛdaya* :

सदाशिवतत्त्वेऽहन्ताच्छादितास्फुटेदन्तामयं विश्वम् ।

i.e., the Universe in *Sadāśiva tattva* is *asphuṭa* or hazy dominated by a clear consciousness of 'I'. *Sadāśiva tattvá* is the first manifestation (*ābhāsa*). For *ābhāsa* or manifestation, there must be a perceiver or knower and perceived or known i.e., a subject and an object. In this universal condition, both are bound to be Consciousness, for there is nothing else than Consciousness. Consciousness in this aspect becomes perceptible to Itself; hence a subject and an object.

4. *Īśvara or Aiśvarya Tattva*

The next stage of the Divine experience is that where *Idam* —the 'This' side of the total experience becomes a little more defined (*sphuṭa*). This is known as *Īśvara Tattva*. It is *unmeṣa* or distinct blossoming of the Universe. At this stage, *jñāna* or knowledge is predominant. There is a clear idea of what is to be created. Rājānaka Ānanda says in his *Vivaraṇa* :

अत्र वेद्यजातस्य स्फुटावभासनात् ज्ञानशक्त्युद्रेकः ।

"As at this stage, the objective side of Experience, the 'This' or the Universe is clearly defined, therefore *jñāna-śakti* is predominant."

Just as an artist has at first a hazy idea of the picture he has to produce, but later a clearer image of the picture begins to emerge in his view, even so at the Sadāśiva stage, the Universe is just a hazy idea, but at the Īśvara stage, it becomes clearer. The experience of Sadāśiva is "I am this". The experience of Iśvara is : "*This* am I."

5. *Sadvidyā or Śuddhavidyā Tattva*

In the *Sadvidyā tattva*, the 'I' and the 'This' side of Experience are equally balanced like the two pans of an evenly held balance (*samadhṛtatulāpuṭanyāyena*). At this stage, Kriyā Śakti is predominant. The 'I' and 'This' are recognised in this state with such equal clarity that while both 'I' and 'This' are still identified, they can be clearly distinguished in thought. The experience of this stage may be called diversity-in-unity *bhedābhedavimarśanātmaka*) i.e., while the 'This' is clearly distinguished from 'I', it is still felt to be a part of the 'I' or Self. Both 'I' and 'This' refer to the same thing (i.e., they have *samanādhikaraṇya*).

In *Śiva tattva*, there is the I-experience (*Aham vimarśa*); in Sadāśiva, there is I-This experience (*Aham-idam vimarśa*); in *Īśvara tattva*, there is This-I experience (*Idamaham vimarśa*). In each of these experiences, the emphasis is on the first term. In *Śuddhavidyā tattva*, there is equal emphasis on both. (*Aham Aham—Idam Idam*. I am I—This is This). Since this experience is intermediate—between the *para* or the higher and *apara* the lower—in which there is a sense of difference, it is called *parāpara daśā*.

It is called *Sadvidyā* or *Śuddhavidyā*, because at this stage the true relation of things is experienced.

Upto this stage, all experience is ideal i.e., in the form of an idea. Hence it is called the perfect or 'pure order' (*Śuddhādhvan*) i.e., a manifestation in which the *svarūpa* or real nature of the Divine is not yet veiled.

II *The Tattvas of the Limited Individual Experience*

6-11. *Māyā and the five Kañcukas*

At this stage, *Māyā tattva* begins its play. From this stage onward there is Aśuddhādhvan or the order in which the real nature of the Divine is concealed. All this happens because of Māyā, and her *kañcukas*. Māyā is derived from the root 'mā', to measure out. That which makes experience measurable i.e., limited and severs 'This' from 'I' and 'I' from 'This' and excludes things from one another is Māyā. Upto Sadvidyā, the experience was Universal; the 'This' meant 'all-this' —the total universe. Under the operation of Māyā, 'this' means merely 'this' different from every thing else. From now on starts *Saṅkoca* or limitation. *Māyā* draws a veil (*āvaraṇa*) on the Self owing to which he forgets his real nature, and thus Māyā generates a sense of difference.*

The products of *Māyā* are the five *kañcukas* or coverings. We may notice them briefly :

(*i*) *Kalā*. This reduces the *sarvakartṛtva* (universal authorship) of the Universal Consciousness and brings about limitation in respect of authorship or efficacy.

(*ii*) *Vidyā*. This reduces the omniscience (*sarvajñatva*) of the Universal Consciousness and brings about limitation in respect of knowledge.

(*iii*) *Rāga*. This reduces the all-satisfaction (*pūrṇatva*) of the Universal and brings about desire for this or that.

(*iv*) *Kāla*. This reduces the eternity (*nityatva*) of the Universal and brings about limitation in respect of time i.e., division of past, present, and future.

(*v*) *Niyati*. This reduces the freedom and pervasiveness (:(*svatantratā* and *vyāpakatva*)) of the Universal, and brings about limitation in respect of cause and space.

III *The Tattvas of the Limited Individual Subject-Object*

12. *Puruṣa*

Śiva thus subjecting Himself to Māyā and putting on the five kañcukas or cloaks which limit His universal knowledge and power becomes Puruṣa or the individual subject. Puruṣa does not merely mean the human person, but every sentient being that is thus limited.

Puruṣa is also known as Aṇu which literally means a point. Point does not mean a spatial point here, for Aṇu being divine in essence cannot be spatial. Puruṣa is called Aṇu because of the limitation of the divine perfection :

पूर्णत्वाभावेन परिमितत्वादणुत्वम् ।

13. *Prakṛti*

While Puruṣa is the subjective manifestation of the 'I am this' experience of Sadvidyā, Prakṛti is the objective

* 'मायाविभेदबुद्धिर्निजांशजातेषु निखिलजीवेषु'

—*Ṣaṭtriṁśattattvasandoha* v.5

manifestation. According to Trika, Prakṛti is the objective effect of Kalā—

वेद्यमात्रं स्फुटं भिन्नं प्रधानं सूयते कला ।—*Tantrāl.*, Āhn. 9

Prakrti is the barest objectivity in contrast with Puruṣa who is Vedaka or Subject. Prakṛti exists in a state of equilibrium of her *guṇas*.

There is a difference between the Sāṅkhya conception of Prakṛti and that of Trika. Sāṅkhya believes that Prakṛti is one and universal for all the Puruṣas. Trika believes that each Puruṣa has a different Prakṛti. Prakṛti is the root or matrix of objectivity.

Prakṛti has three *guṇas*—threads or constituents. viz., Sattva, Rajas and Tamas (producing respectively sukha, duḥkha, and moha). Prakṛti is the Śāntā Śakti of Śiva and the *guṇas* Sattva, Rajas, and Tamas are the gross forms of His Śaktis of Jñāna, Icchā, and Kriyā respectively.

Puruṣa is the Experient (*bhoktā*) and Prakṛti is the experienced (*bhogyā*).

IV. *The Tattvas of Mental Operation*

14-16—*Buddhi, Ahaṁkāra, and Manas*

Prakṛti differentiates into *antaḥkaraṇa* (the psychic apparatus), *indriyas* (senses) and *bhūtas* (matter).

We shall first take up *antaḥkaraṇa*. It means literally the inner instrument i.e., the psychic apparatus of the individual. It consists of the *tattvas* by means of which there is mental operation, viz., Buddhi, Ahaṁkāra, and Manas.

1. Buddhi is the first *tattva* of Prakṛti. It is the ascertaining intelligence (*vyavasāyātmikā*). The objects that are reflected in Buddhi are of two kinds: (a) external e.g., a jar, the reflection of which is received through the eye etc., (b) internal—the images built out of the *saṁskāras* (the impressions left behind on the mind).

2. *Ahaṁkāra*. This is the product of Buddhi. It is the I-consciousness and the power of self-appropriation.

3. *Manas*. It is the product of Ahaṁkāra. It cooperates with the senses in building up perceptions, and it builds up images and concepts.

V-VII. *The Tattvas of Sensible Experience* : 17-31

1. The five powers of sense-perception—Jñānendriyas or Buddhīndriyas—they are the products of Ahaṁkāra. The five powers are those of

(i) smelling (*ghrāṇendriya*)
(ii) tasting (*rasanendriya*)
(iii) seeing (*cakṣurindriya*)
(iv) feeling by touch (*sparśanendriya*)
(v) hearing (*śravaṇendriya*)

2. The five *karmendriyas* or powers of action. These are also products of Ahaṁkāra. These are the powers of :

(i) speaking (*vāgindriya*)
(ii) handling (*hastendriya*)
(iii) locomotion (*pādendriya*)
(iv) excreting (*pāyvindriya*)
(v) sexual action and restfulness (*upasthendriya*).

The *indriyas* are not sense-organs but *powers* which operate through the sense-organs. In common parlance, they are used for sense-organs also.

3. The five *tanmātras* or primary elements of perception. These are also products of Ahaṁkāra. Literally *tanmātra* means 'that only'. These are the general elements of the particulars of sense-perception. They are :

(i) Sound-as-such (*Śabda-tanmātra*)
(ii) Touch-as-such (*Sparśa-tanmātra*)
(iii) Colour-as-such (*Rūpa-tanmātra*)
(iv) Flavour-as-such (*Rasa-tanmātra*)
(v) Odour-as-such (*Gandha-tanmātra*)

VIII. *The Tattvas of Materiality*

32-36. *The Five Bhūtas*

The five gross elements or the pañca-*Mahābhūtas* are the products of the five *tanmātras*.

(i)	Ākāśa is produced from		Śabda-tanmātra.
(ii)	Vāyu is	,,	Sparśa-tanmātra.
(iii)	Teja (Agni)	,,	Rūpa-tanmātra.

(iv) Āpas is produced from Rasa-tanmātra
(v) Pṛthivī ,, ,, Gandha-tanmātra.

3. *Svātantryavāda* and *Ābhāsavāda*

Svātantryavāda

The Absolute in this system is known as Cit or Paramaśiva or Maheśvara. It is called Maheśvara not in the ordinary sense of God as the first cause that is to be inferred from the order and design in Nature. It is called Maheśvara because of its absolute sovereignty of Will, *sva-tantratā* or *svātantrya*. This absolute Sovereignty or Free Will is not a blind force but the *svabhāva* (own being) of the Universal Consciousness (Cit). It is this sovereign Free Will that brings about the objectification of its ideation. It is free inasmuch as it does not depend on any thing external to it: it is free and potent to bring about anything. It is beyond all the categories of time, space, causality etc., for these owe their origin to it.

चितिः प्रत्यवमर्शात्मा परावाक्स्वरसोदिता ।
स्वातंत्र्यमेतन्मुख्यम् तदैश्वर्यं परमात्मनः ॥

—Īśvara. Pr. I, p. 203-4

"The Divine Power is known as Citi. Its essence is Self-Consciousness. It is also known as Parā Vāk. It is in itself ever present, eternal. It is *svātantrya*. It is the main Power of the Supreme Self."

Parā Vāk, Vimarśa, Aiśvarya etc. are only the synonyms of Svātantrya.

सा स्फुरत्ता महासत्ता देशकालाविशेषिणी ।
सैषा सारतया प्रोक्ता हृदयं परमेष्ठिनः ॥

—Īśvara. Pr. I p. 207-8

"This *Citi* or power of Universal Consciousness is the inner, creative flash which, though in itself unchanging, is the source of all apparent change; it is *mahāsattā* or absolute being inasmuch as it is free to be anything, it is the source of all that can be said to exist in any way. It is beyond the determinations of space and time. In essence. this Free, Sovereign Will may be said to be the very heart or nucleus of the Divine Being."

Svâtantrya or Māheśvarya means Absolute Sovereignty or Freedom of Will. It connotes unimpeded activity of the Divine Will and is an expression of Self-Consciousness.

"स्वातंत्र्य च नाम यथेच्छं तत्रेच्छाप्रसरस्य अविघात: ।"

"Svātantrya means the Power to do according to one's will; it is the unimpeded, unrestrained flow of expression of the Divine Will."

Svātantryavāda or the doctrine of the Absolute Sovereignty and Freedom of the Divine Will to express or manifest itself in any way it likes has been beautifully explained in the following words by Abhinavagupta :

"तस्मादनपह्नवनीय: प्रकाशविमर्शात्मा संवित्स्वभाव: परमशिवो भगवान् स्वातंत्र्यादेव रुद्रादिस्थावरान्तप्रमातृरूपतया नीलसुखादिप्रमेयरूपतया च अनतिरिक्तयापि अतिरिक्तया इव स्वरूपानाच्छादिकया संविद्रूपनान्तरीयकस्वातंत्र्यमहिम्ना प्रकाशत इति अयं स्वातंत्र्यवाद: प्रोन्मीलित:"

—Īś. Pr. V.V. Pt. I, p. 9.

"Therefore the Lord, Parama Śiva (the Absolute Reality) whose own being is Consciousness of the nature of Prakāśa and Vimarśa, who as the undeniable, ever-present Reality appears as subject from Rudra down to immovable entities, as objects like blue, pleasure etc. which appear as if separate, though in essence they are not separate, through the glorious might of *Svātantrya* (Free Will) which is inseparable from Saṁvit (universal Consciousness) and which does not conceal in any way the real nature of the Supreme. This is the exposition of *Svātantrya-vāda* (the doctrine of Svātantrya)."

Ābhāsavāda

From the point of view of the creativity of Ultimate Reality, this philosophy is known as *svātantryavāda*; from the point of view of its manifestation, it is known as *ābhāsavāda*..

In the ultimate Reality, the entire manifested variety is in perfect unity, an undifferentiated mass just as the variegated plumage of the peacock with its beautiful, rich colour lies in a state of undifferentiated mass in the plasma of its egg. This is called in this system the analogy of the plasma of the peacock's egg (*mayūrāṇḍarasanyāya*).

The underlying principle of all manifestation is *Cit* or pure Universal Consciousness. The world of ever-changing appearances is only an expression of Cit or Saṁvid. All that appears in any form whether as an object or subject or knowledge or means of knowledge or senses, all that exists in any way is only an *ābhāsa*—a manifestation of the Universal Consciousness. The word ābhāsa = *ā* i.e., *iṣat* (saṅkocena); *bhāsaḥ* = *bhāsanam* or *prakāśanā*. So *ābhāsa* is manifestation or appearance in a limited way. Every kind of manifestation has some sort of limitation. Every thing in existence is a configuration of *ābhāsas*.

"दर्पणबिम्बे यद्वन् नगरग्रामादिचित्रमविभागि ।
भातिविभागेनैव च परस्परं दर्पणादपि च ॥
विमलतमपरमभैरवबोधात् तद्वत् विभागशून्यमपि ।
अन्योन्यं च ततोऽपि च विभक्तमाभाति जगदेतत् ॥

—Paramārthasāra, 12-13

"Just as in a clear mirror, varied images of city, village etc. appear as different from one another and from the mirror though they are non-different from the mirror, even so the world, though non-different from the purest consciousness of Parama Śiva, appears as different both in respect of its varied objects and that Universal Consciousness."

Ābhāsas are explained on the analogy of reflection in a mirror. Just as reflection in a mirror is not in any way different from the mirror, but appears as something different, even so *ābhāsas* are not different from Śiva and yet appear as different. Just as in a mirror, a village, a tree, river etc. appear as different from the mirror, but are, truly speaking, nothing different from it, even so the world reflected in the Universal Consciousness is nothing different from it.

Two exceptions have, however, to be noted in the analogy of the mirror. Firstly, in the case of the mirror, there is an external object that is reflected: in the case of Maheśvara or Universal Consciousness, it is its own ideation that is reflected. In the case of the mirror, there is an external light owing to which reflection is possible; in the case of the

Universal Consciousness, it is its own light; it is the Light of all lights; it does not require any external light.

Secondly, the mirror being non-conscious does not know the reflections within itself, but the Universal Consciousness knows its own ideation which appears in itself. Ābhāsas are nothing but the ideation of the Universal Consciousness appearing as external to the empirical subject.

> अन्तर्विभाति सकलं जगदात्मनीह
> यद्वद् विचित्ररचना मकुरान्तराले ।
> बोधः पुनर्निजविमर्शनसारयुक्त्या
> विश्वं परामृशति नो मकुरस्तथा ॥
> —quoted by Yogarāja in Paramārthasāra, p. 39

"Just as a variety of objects appears, within a mirror, even so the entire universe appears within Consciousness or the Self. Consciousness, however, owing to its power of *vimarśa* or Self-consciousness knows the world, not so the mirror its objects."

All *ābhāsas* rise like waves in the sea of the Universal Consciousness. Just as there is neither loss nor gain to the sea with the rise and disappearance of the waves, even so there is neither loss nor gain to the Universal Consciousness because of the appearance and disappearance of the *ābhāsas*. Ābhāsas appear and disappear but the underlying Consciousness is unchanging.

The *ābhāsas* are nothing but external projection of the ideation of the Divine.

> "चिदात्मैव हि देवोऽन्तःस्थितमिच्छावशाद्बहिः ।
> योगीव निरुपादानमर्थजातं प्रकाशयेत् ॥"
> —Iś.Pr. I. 5. 7

"The Divine Being whose essence is *Cit* (Universal Consciousness) makes the collection of objects that are internally contained appear outside by His Will without any external material even as a Yogī (makes his mental objects appear outside by his mere will)."

The Divine Being does not create like a pot-maker shaping clay into pots. Sṛṣṭi only means manifesting outside what is contained within. The Divine does not require any external material for this. This is accomplished by His mere Will power.

Things which are identical with the Divine Being's knowledge or *jñāna* appear by His Will as *jñeya* or objects, things which are identical with His Self or 'I' appear as 'this' or the universe. To the empirical subjects, they appear as something external.

It is the Universal Consciousness itself that appears in the form of subjects and objects. Therefore, this appearance cannot be called false. This appearance makes no difference to the Fullness or Perfection of the Universal Consciousness.

Svātantryavāda of this philosophy stands in contradistinction to *vivartavāda* and *ābhāsavāda* to *pariṇāmavāda*.

4. *Ṣaḍadhvā*

From another point of view, viz., of *parāśakti*, manifestation or creative descent is described in the following way :

There is an unbounded potency or basic continuum of power which is known as *nāda*. This condenses itself into dynamic point or centre, called *bindu*. The condensation is not a process in time or space. This is the source of all manifestation. In the highest stage of manifestation, *vācaka* and *vācya* (the indicator and the indicated, the word and object) are one. Then there are six *adhvās*, paths or steps of creative descent. These are known as Ṣaḍadhvā. First of all, there is the polarity of *varṇa* and *kalā*. Primarily, Kalā is that aspect of Reality by which it manifests itself as power for evolving universes. The transcendental aspect of Reality or Parama Śiva is known as *niṣkala*, for it transcends Kalā or creativity. The immanent aspect of Śiva is *sakala* for it is concerned with creativity.

But in the present context, coming after *nāda-bindu*, *kalā* means a phase, an aspect of creativity. It is here that things begin to differentiate from an integrated whole. *Vācaka* and *Vācya* (index and object) which were one at the *parāvāk* stage begin to differentiate. The first *adhvā* or step of this differentiation is the polarity of *varṇa* and *kalā*. As Svāmī Pratyagātmānanda Sarasvatī puts it, *varṇa* in this context does not mean letter or colour or class, but a 'function-form' of the object projected from *bindu*. *Varṇa*, therefore, connotes 'the characteristic measure-index of the function form associated with the object'. *Varṇa* is the 'function-form', *Kalā* is 'predicable'.

The next *adhvā* in the subtle plane is that of *mantra* and *tattva*. *Mantra* is the 'appropriate function-form' or 'basic formula' of the next creative descent viz., *tattva*. *Tattva* is the inherent principle or the source and origin of subtle structural forms.

The third and final polarity is that of *pada* and *bhuvana*. *Bhuvana* is the universe as it appears to apprehending centres like ourselves. *Pada* is the actual formulation of that universe by mind reaction and speech.

The Ṣaḍadhvā may be briefly indicated in the following table :—

Vācaka or Śabda	Vācya or artha
Varṇa	Kalā
Mantra	Tattva
Pada	Bhuvana

The *trika* or triad on the *vācaka* side is known as *kālādhvā*; the *trika* or triad on the *vācya* side is known as *deśādhvā*.

Varṇādhvā is of the nature of *pramā*. It is the resting place of *prameya* (object), *pramāṇa* (means of knowledge) and *pramātā* (experient). *Varṇa* is of two kinds ; *non-māyīya* and *māyīya*. The *māyīya varṇas* arise out of the *non-māyīya*. The *non-māyīya varṇas* are pure, natural, without limitation and innumerable. The Vācaka Śakti (indicative power) of *non-māyīya varṇas* is inherent in the *māyīya varṇas* even as power of heating is inherent in fire.

The kalās are five in number, viz., (1) Nivṛtti *kalā*, (2) Pratiṣṭhā kalā, (3) Vidyā kalā, (4) Śāntā or Śānti kalā, and (5) Śāntyatītā kalā.

As for the *tattvas* and *bhuvanas* contained in each kalā, see the diagram under Note no. 174 and the details given below the diagram. According to Abhinavagupta, there are 118 *bhuvanas*. According to some others, there are 224 *bhuvanas*.

5. *Comparison and Contrast with Śaṁkara's Advaitavāda*

Śaṁkara's philosophy is known as *Śānta brahmavāda* or *Kevalādvaitavāda* or sometimes, as *Māyā-Vedānta-vāda*. The Śaiva philosophy of Kashmir is known as *Īśvarādvayavāda* or *Pratyabhijñā* or *Trika* philosophy. Since Śaṁkara believes that *brahman* has no activity, his philosophy is mostly characterized as *Śāntabrahmavāda* or the philosophy of inactive *brahman* by the Śaiva philosophers.

The first salient difference between *Śāntabrahmavāda* and *Īśvarādvayavāda* is that according to the former the characteristic of *cit* or *brahman* is only *prakāśa* or *jñāna*, whereas according to the latter it is both *prakāśa* and *vimarśa*. In other words, according to Śaṁkara, the characteristic of *brahman* is only *jñāna* (knowledge); according to *Īśvarādvayavāda*, it is both *jñātṛtva* or (knowledge) and *kartṛtva* (activity). Śaṁkara thinks that *kriyā* or activity belongs only to *jīva* or the empirical subject and not to *brahman*. He takes *kriyā* in a very narrow sense. Śaiva philosophy takes *kartṛtva* or activity in a wide sense. According to it even *jñāna* is an activity of the Divine. Without activity, *Cit* or the Divine being would be inert and incapable of bringing about anything. Since Parama Śiva is *svatantra* (i.e., has sovereign Free Will), therefore is he a *kartā* (doer). As Pāṇini puts it स्वतन्त्रः कर्ता "only a free-willed being is a doer". *Svātantrya* (Free Will) and *kartṛtva* (the power to act) are practically the same thing.

In *Śāntabrahmavāda*, *brahman* is entirely inactive. When *brahman* is associated with *avidyā*, it becomes Īśvara and is endowed with the power to act. The real activity belongs to *avidyā*. The activity of Īśvara ceases when he is dissociated from *avidyā*. Śaṁkara says categorically :

"तदेवमविद्यात्मकोपाधिपरिच्छेदापेक्षमेवेश्वरस्येश्वरत्वं सर्वज्ञत्वं सर्वशक्तित्वं च, न परमार्थतो विद्ययापास्तसर्वोपाधिस्वरूपे आत्मनीशित्रीशितव्यसर्वज्ञत्वादि व्यवहार उपपद्यते" (Br. Sū.2. 1.14)

"Thus the potency of Īśvara, his omniscience and omnipotence are contingent upon the limitation caused by the condition or association of *avidyā* (primal ignorance). In the highest sense, when all conditions are removed by *vidyā* (spiritual illumination) from the Ātman, the use of potency, omniscience etc. would become inappropriate for it." So all activity in the case of Īśvara is, according to Śaṁkara, due to *avidyā*.

On the other hand, *jñātṛtva* and *kartṛtva* (knowledge and activity) are according to Īśvarādvayavāda, the very nature of the Supreme. Never can the Supreme be thought of without His activity. In this philosophy, activity is not an adjunct of Īśvara as in Śaṁkara, but His very specific nature. In general terms, His activity may be summed up in the five-fold act of emanation or projection (*sṛṣṭi*), maintenance (*sthiti*) withdrawal (*saṁhāra*), concealment of the real nature (*vilaya*), and grace (*anugraha*). He performs these five acts eternally even when he assumes the form of an empirical ego (*jīva*). According to Īśvarādvayavāda, Śiva is *pañcakṛtyakārī* (always performing five-fold act). According to Śaṁkara, *brahman* is *niṣkriya* (without any activity). Maheśvarānanda says that inactive *brahman* is as good as unreal.

"तथाहि परमेश्वरस्य ह्ययमेवासाधारणस्वभावो यत् सर्वदा सृष्ट्यादिपञ्चकृत्यकारित्वम् । एतदनङ्गीकाराद्धि मायावेदान्तादिनिर्णीतस्यात्मनः स्वस्फुरणामोदमान्द्यलक्षणमसत्कल्पत्वापतितम् ।"(Mahārthamañjarī, p.52)
"This is the specific nature of Parameśvara (Highest Lord) that He always performs the five-fold act of *sṛṣṭi* etc. If this (i.e., activity) is not accepted, Ātmā as defined by Māyā-Vedānta etc., characterized by the want of the slightest trace of stir or activity would be as good as unreal."

Īśvarādvayavāda also accepts *avidyā* or *māyā*, but, according to it, *avidyā* or *māyā* is not something which happens to affect Īśvara; it is rather Īśvara's own voluntarily self-imposed limitation of Himself by His own *śakti* (power). According to Śaṁkara, *brahman* is entirely inactive; all activity is due to *māyā*. According to Īśvarādvayavāda, activity belongs to Īśvara; *māyā* derives only its activity from Him.

Secondly, *māyā*, according to *Śāntabrahmavāda* is *anirvacanīya* (indefinable), but according to Īśvarādvayavāda, *māyā* being the *śakti* of Īśvara or Śiva is real and brings about multiplicity and sense of difference.

According to Śāntabrahmavāda, *viśva* or the universe is *mithyā* or unreal. According to Īśvarādvayavāda, the universe is perfectly real; it is simply a display of Īśvara's power. Since *śakti* is real, the universe which has been brought about by *śakti* is also real. Since Śaṁkara considers *māyā* as neither real nor unreal (सदसद्भ्यामनिर्वचनीया), his non-dualism is exclusive, but the non-dual Śaiva philosophy considers *māyā* as *śiva-mayī* (an aspect of Śiva), therefore the Śaiva non-dualism is integral, all-inclusive. If *brahman* is real and *māyā* is some indeterminate force—neither real nor unreal as Śaṁkara maintains, then there would be a tinge of dualism in Śaṁkara's philosophy.

Again, according to Īśvarādvayavāda, even in the state of the empirical ego or *jīva*, the five-fold act of Śiva continues; according to Śāntabrahmavāda, *ātmā* (self) even in the state of the empirical ego is *niṣkriya* or inactive. Whatever activity there is belongs to *buddhi*.

According to Śaṁkara's *vivartavāda*, all manifestation is only name and form (*nāma-rūpa*) and cannot be regarded as real in the true sense of the word. According to Īśvarādvayavāda, the *ābhāsas* are real in the sense that they are aspects of the ultimately real or Parama Śiva. Though they do not exist in Parama Śiva in the same way in which limited beings experience them, they exist in Parama Śiva as His experience or ideation. So the *ābhāsas* are in essence real. What constitutes the ideation of the Real cannot itself be unreal.

Finally, in *mukti* (liberation), the world, according to Śaṁkara, is annulled; in Śaiva philosophy, it appears as a gleam of Śiva-consciousness or an expression of the wondrous delight of self-consciousness.

We may summarize the views of the two systems in a tabular form.

	Śāntabrahmavāda	*Īśvarādvayavāda*
1.	*Cit* or *brahman* is only *prakāśa* (light) or *jñāna* (knowledge). It is *niṣkriya* (inactive)	Cit is both *prakāśa* and *vimarśa* (light and activity). Therefore it has both *jñātṛtva* (knowledge) and *kartṛtva* (doership). Generally speaking, it has five-fold activity.
2.	Activity belongs only to *māyā* or *avidyā*. Īśvara assumes activity only when	Maheśvara has *svātantrya*. Therefore activity belongs to Him. Māyā is not something

	He is affected by *avidyā* or *māyā*.	which affects Maheśvara or Śiva. Māyā is His own *Śakti* by which, He brings about multiplicity and sense of difference.
3.	Māyā is *anirvacanīya* (indefinable)	Māyā being the *śakti* of the Divine is perfectly real.
4.	Māyā being indefinable is loosely associated with Īśvara and is, in the last analysis, unreal. Māyā seems to play the role of a separate principle. Śaṁkara's non-dualism is, therefore exclusive.	Māyā is *Śiva-mayī* or *cinmayī* and is thus Śiva's own *śakti*. It is not a separate principle. Therefore, Śaiva non-dualism is inclusive and integral.
5.	In the case of the empirical ego or *jīva* also, the *ātman* is inactive. All activity belongs to *buddhi*, the product of *prakṛti*	Even in the case of *jīva*, the five-fold activity of Śiva never ceases.
6.	The universe is *mithyā* or unreal. Manifestation is only *nāma-rūpa* and cannot be regarded as real in the true sense. Śaṁkara's non-dualism is exclusive of the universe.	The universe is *śiva-rūpa* and therefore real. It is a display of the glory of the Divine. Ābhāsas being the ideation of Śiva cannot be false. Śaiva philosophy is thus inclusive of the universe and real non-dualism.
7.	In liberation, the universe is annulled.	In liberation, the universe appears as a form of Śiva-consciousness or real I-consciousness.
8.	According to Śāṁkara Vedānta, *avidyā* is removed by *vidyā*, and when this happens, there is *mukti* or liberation. Vidyā is the result of *śravaṇa*, *manana*, and *nididhyāsana*.	According to non-dualistic Śaiva philosophy, there are two kinds of *ajñāna*, viz., *pauruṣa ajñāna* which is inherent in the puruṣa or aṇu and *bauddha ajñāna* which is intellectual. By *Vidyā* only *bauddha ajñāna*

can be removed; *pauruṣa ajñāna* will still remain. Such a person will be landed only in blank abstractions, he will not realize *Śivatva* or divinization. *Pauruṣa ajñāna* has also to be removed. This can be removed only by *śaktipāta* which comes about either by the dīkṣā (initiation)) imparted by a self-realized *guru* (spiritual director) or by direct divine grace.

6. *The Individual Self or Jiva*

The individual according to this system is not simply a psycho-physical being but something more. His physical aspect consists of the five *mahābhūtas* or gross elements highly organised. This is known as his *sthūlaśarira*. He has also the psychic apparatus known as *antaḥkaraṇa* (the inner instrument) consisting of *buddhi, ahaṁkāra* and *manas.*

Buddhi, ahaṁkāra and manas together with the five *tanmātras* form a group of eight which is known as *puryaṣṭaka*. This is the *sūkṣmaśarīra* in which the soul leaves the body at the time of death.

There also works in him *prāṇa śakti*. This is the divine *śakti* working both in the universe and the individual. It is by this *prāṇa śakti* that everything is sustained and maintained.

There is also *kuṇḍalinī* that is a form or expression of *śakti*. This lies dormant in the normal human being.

Finally there is *caitanya* or Śiva in the centre of his being that is his very Self.

Though intrinsically the Self of man is Śiva, he becomes an *aṇu* or a limited individual because of *āṇava mala*.

7. *Bondage*

The bondage of the individual is due to innate ignorance which is known as *āṇava mala*. It is the primary limiting condition which reduces the universal consciousness to an *aṇu* or a limited aspect. It comes about by the limitation of the *Icchā Śakti* of the Supreme. It is owing to this that the *jīva* considers himself a separate entity, cut off from the universal stream of consciousness. It is consciousness of self-limitation.

Coming in association with the categories of the *aśuddha adhvā* or the order of the extrinsic manifestation, he becomes further limited by *māyīya mala* and *kārma mala*. *Māyīya mala* is the limiting condition brought about by *māyā*. It is *bhinna-vedya-prathā* — that which brings about the consciousness of difference owing to the differing limiting adjuncts of the body etc. This comes about by the limitation of the *jñāna śakti* of the Supreme.

It is by these *malas* that the individual is in bondage whirled about from one form of existence to another.

8. *Liberation*

Liberation according to this system means the *re*-cognition (*pratyabhijñā*) of one's true nature which means in other words the attainment of *akṛtrima-aham-vimarśa* — the original, innate, pure I-consciousness. The following verse of Utpaladeva gives an idea of pure I-Consciousness.

अहं प्रत्यवमर्शो यो विमर्शात्मापि वाग्वपुः ।
नासौ विकल्पः, स ह्युक्तो द्वयापेक्षी विनिश्चयः ॥

—Īś. Pr. I. 6.1.

The pure I-consciousness is not of the nature of *vikalpa*, for *vikalpa* requires a second i.e., all *vikalpa* is relational. The normal, psychological I-Consciousness is relational i.e., the Self-Consciousness is in contrast with the not-Self. The pure I-consciousness is not of this relational type. It is *immediate awareness*. When one has this consciousness, one knows one's real nature. This is what is meant by liberation. As Abhinavagupta puts it :

मोक्षो हि नाम नैवान्यः स्वरूपप्रथनं हि तत् ।

—Tantrāloka. I. p. 192.

Mokṣa (liberation) is nothing else but the awareness of one's true nature.

By this real I-consciousness, one attains Cidānanda — the bliss of the cit or Universal Consciousness. The *citta* or the individual mind is now transformed into *Cit* or Universal consciousness (vide Sūtra 13 of Pr. Hṛ.). The attainment of this pure I-consciousness is also the attainment of Śiva-Consciousness in which the entire universe appears as I or Śiva.

According to this system, the highest form of *ānanda* or bliss is *jagadānanda* — the bliss of the world in which the whole world appears to the liberated soul as *Cit* or Śiva.

This liberation cannot be achieved by mere logic-chopping or intellectual pyrotechnic. It comes by *Śaktipāta* (the descent of Divine *Śakti*) or *anugraha* i.e., Divine grace.

Śaktipāta or Anugraha

Those who, owing to the saṁskāras of previous birth, are very advanced souls receive *tīvra* or intense *śaktipāta*. They are liberated without much *sādhanā* or *praxis*.

Those who are less qualified receive *madhyama śaktipāta*. This induces them to seek a *guru* or spiritual preceptor, to get initiation and practise *yoga*. In due course, they get liberation.

Those who are still less qualified receive *manda* (moderate) *śaktipāta*. This creates in them genuine eagerness for spiritual knowledge and meditation. They will also get liberation in course of time.

Upāyas

But grace is not the outcome of caprice. It has to be earned by moral and spiritual discipline. The means of earning grace have been divided under four broad heads, viz., Āṇavopāya, Śāktopāya, Śāmbhavopāya, and Anupāya. These *upāyas* are recommended to get rid of the *malas* so that one may become fit for receiving grace.

Āṇavopāya is the means whereby the individual utilizes his own karaṇas or instruments as means for his transformation for Self-realization. It includes disciplines concerning the regulation of *prāṇa*, rituals, concentration on one's chosen deity etc. Ultimately, it brings about Self-realization by the unfolding of *madhya-dhāma* or *suṣumnā*. It is also known as *kriyopāya*, because *Kriyā* — such as repetition of a mantra and the practice of rituals etc. — plays an important part in it. This is also known as *bhedopāya*, because this discipline starts with a sense of *bheda* or difference.

Śāktopāya is concerned with those psychological practices which transform the inner forces, and bring about in the individual *samāveśa* or immersion of the individual consciousness in the divine. In this mostly *mantra śakti* comes into play by which the individual acquires *prātibha jñāna* or true knowledge; gradually his feeling of duality gets less and less and his consciousness merges in *parā-saṁvid*. In this discipline one has to meditate something like this "I am Śiva", "The whole universe is only an expansion of my true Self".

In *āṇavopāya*, the senses, *prāṇa* and *manas* are pressed into service; in *śāktopāya*, it is *manas* only that functions actively. It is also known as *jñānopāya*, because mental activities play an important role in it. It is also known as *bhedābheda-upāya*, because it is based both on difference and identity. By this, the *kuṇḍalinī* rises up from *mūlādhāra* without much effort for the control of *prāṇa* and brings about Self-realization.

Śāmbhavopāya is meant for advanced aspirants who by meditating on *Śivatattva* attain to His consciousness. This is the path of 'constant awareness'. One starts with the analysis of *pañca-kṛtya*, *sādhanā* of *vikalpa-kṣaya*, and the practice of the consciousness that the universe is only reflection of *cit*, but later even these have to be given up. This leads easily to pure I-consciousness.

Anupāya can hardly be called an *upāya*. This depends entirely on *anugraha* or grace. This grace may come through one word of the *guru* (spiritual director) and light may dawn upon the aspirant and thus he may acquire an experience of the real self in a trice or divine grace may be showered on him directly and he may instantly realize his Self. The prefix 'an' in *anupāya* has been explained by some in the sense of *iṣat* or very little. In this sense *anupāya* means very little or nominal effort on the part of the aspirant. In both cases, *anupāya* connotes realization, solely through very intense grace (*tīvratama śaktipāta*). Sometimes by the very sight of a person who has acquired self-realization, an aspirant receives illumination, and is transformed.

Anupāya is generally designated as *ānandopāya*.

Kṣemarāja says that by the development of the *madhya* or centre, one attains *cidānanda* or bliss of the Supreme consciousness. This *madhya* is to be conceived separately from the point of view of the above three *upāyas*. From the point of view of the *āṇavopāya*, '*madhya*' is the *suṣumnā nāḍi* between the *iḍā* and *piṅgalā* that has to be unfolded. From the point of view of *śāktopāya*, '*madhya*' is the *parā-saṁvid* that has to be reached. From the point of view of *Śāmbhavopāya* it is *akṛtrima aham* or the pure I-consciousness that is the '*madhya*' or centre of everything. It is the *madhya* that has to be attained by one of the above means.

For the unfoldment of *madhya*, Kṣemarāja recommends *vikalpa-kṣaya*, *śakti-saṅkoca*, *śakti-vikāsa*, *vāha-ccheda*, and the practice of *ādyanta-koṭi* (for details, see Sūtra 18).

Of these, *vikalpa-kṣaya* is *śāmbhavopāya*, *śaktisaṅkoca* and *vikāsa* are *śāktopāya*, and *vāha-ccheda* and *ādyanta-koṭinibhālana* are *āṇavopāya*.

Pratyabhijñā lays the greatest stress on the meditation on *pañca-kṛtya* and the practice of *vikalpa-kṣaya*. It maintains that the five-fold act of Śiva, viz., *sṛṣṭi*, *sthiti*, *saṁhāra*, *vilaya* and *anugraha* is going on constantly even in the individual. The aspirant should constantly dwell on the esoteric meaning of this five-fold act in order to rise to higher consciousness. The mental perception of the individual with reference to a particular place and time is the *sṛṣṭi* in him, the retention and enjoyment of what he perceives is the *sthiti* or preservation. At the time of the delight of I-consciousness, it is absorbed in consciousness. This is *saṁhāra*. When even after its being withdrawn, its impression is about to rise into consciousness again, it corresponds to *vilaya*. When it is completely absorbed into *Cit* or true Self by the process of *haṭha-pāka*, it is *anugraha*. (Sūtra 11 may be consulted for details). This practice qualifies the aspirant for pure *cidānanda*.

Another method is *vikalpa-kṣaya*. The mind is the happy hunting-ground of all kinds of ideas that rise one after another like waves upon the sea. We get involved in these ideas and are unable to get behind them to the placidity of the underlying consciousness. The practice of *vikalpa-kṣaya* is recommended for getting rid of *kṣobha* or mental agitation, and recapturing the underlying consciousness, on the surface of which the *vikalpas* have their play. This cannot be done by force, for that creates resistance. This can be achieved only by *alert passivity*, by relaxing the *citta* or mind, by not thinking of anything in particular, and yet not losing awareness.

By these practices, one acquires *samāveśa* or immersion into the divine consciousness. In order that this *samāveśa* may be full, perfect and an enduring experience, one has to practise *Krama-mudrā* (for details of Krama-mudrā, see Sūtra 19). By Krama-mudrā, the experience of identification of the individual consciousness with the Universal Consciousness has to be carried out into the experience of the outer world. This system does not believe that *samāveśa* to be complete which lasts only so long as *samādhi* (contemplation) lasts, and disappears after one rises from that state. It believes that that is perfect *samāveśa* in which even after getting up from the contemplative state, it continues, and the world no longer appears as mere 'earth, earthy', but as 'apparelled in celestial light', as an expression, and play of the Universal Consciousness, and the aspirant feels himself also as nothing but that consciousness. Then the world is no longer something to be shunned, but an eternal delight (*jagadānanda*). Then does one truly acquire *akṛtrima-aham-vimarśa* — pure I-consciousness in which the world does not stand over against the I in opposition but is the expression of that I itself.

This is the conception of *jīvan-mukti* in this system. The world-process starts from the pure I-consciousness of Śiva. At the level of man that I-consciousness gets identified with its physical and psychic coverings, and the world stands over against it as something different *toto caelo*. The task of man is to re-capture that pure I-consciousness in which it and the universe are one.

Surely, such a stage cannot be reached all at once. The system visualizes a hierarchy of experients who rise gradually in the evolutionary process to the pure I-consciousness of Śiva.

The normal individual is known as *sakala.* He has all the three *malas* — *kārma, māyīya* and *āṇava.* After many rebirths during which he is the plaything of Nature—both physical and psychic, he is seized with psychic fever and tries to know the *whence* and the *whither* of this life. This is the first expression of the *anugraha* of Śiva.

If he is not very cautious and indulges in lower kinds of *yoga,* he may become a *pralayākala.* He is free from *kārma mala,* and has only *māyiya* and *āṇava mala,* but he has neither *jñāna* nor *kriyā.* This is not a desirable state. At the time of *pralaya* or withdrawal of the universe, every *sakala* becomes a *pralayākala.*

Vijñānākala is an experient of a higher stage. He has risen above *māyā* but is still below *Śuddha Vidyā.* He is free from the *kārma* and *māyīya malas* but has still *āṇava mala.* He has *jñāna* and *icchā,* but no *kriyā.*

Above the *vijnānākala* are the experients in successive ascent known as Mantra, Mantreśvara, Mantra-maheśvara and Śiva-pramātā. These are free from all the three *malas,* but they have varying experience of unity consciousness (for details, the chart in Note no. 39 may be seen).

It is only to the Śiva-pramātā that every thing appears as Śiva.

Pure I-consciousness is the *fons et origo* of the entire world process.

Involution starts from the pure I-consciousness of Śiva. Evolution gets back to the same pure consciousness, but the pilgrim goes back to his home, enriched with the experience of the splendour of Śiva he has had on the way. Veil after veil lifts, and he is now poised in the heart of Reality. He may now well exclaim in the words of Abhinavagupta :

स्वतंत्रः स्वच्छात्मा स्फुरति सततं चेतसि शिवः
पराशक्तिश्चेयं करणसरणिप्रान्तमुदिता ।
तदा भोगैकात्मा स्फुरति च समस्तं जगदिदम्
न जाने कुत्रायं ध्वनिरनुपतेत् संसृतिरिति ॥

—quoted in Mahārthamañjarī p. 25.

"It is Śiva Himself, of un-impeded Will and pellucid consciousness, who is ever sparkling in my heart. It is His highest Śakti Herself that is ever playing on the edge of my senses. The entire world gleams as the wondrous delight of pure I-consciousness. Indeed I know not what the sound 'world' is supposed to refer to."

ANALYSIS OF CONTENTS

Sūtra 1 : *The absolute Citi (Consciousness) out of its own free will is the cause of the siddhi of the universe.*

Universe in this context means everything from Sadāśiva down to the earth.

Siddhi means bringing into manifestation, maintenance, and withdrawal.

Citi—The absolute consciousness alone is the power that brings about manifestation. Māyā, Prakṛti is not the cause of manifestation. Inasmuch as it (*Citi*) is the source of both subject, object, and pramāṇa (means of proof), no means of proof can prove it (i.e. it is its own source).

Siddhi may be taken in another sense also. It may mean *bhoga* (experience) and *mokṣa* (liberation). Of these also the absolute freedom of the ultimate divine consciousness is the cause.

The word '*hetu*' in the *sūtra* means not only cause in which sense it has been already interpreted above. It also means 'means'. So *Citi* is also the means of the individual's ascension to the highest consciousness where he becomes identified with the divine consciousness.

Citi has been used in the singular to show that it is unlimited by space, time etc. It has been called *svatantra* (of free will) in order to show that it by itself is powerful to bring about the universe without the aid of Māyā etc.

Citi is, therefore, the cause of manifestation, the means of rising to Śiva, and also the highest end. This Sūtra strikes the key-note of the entire book.

Sūtra 2 : *By the power of her own free will does she (Citi) unfold the universe upon her own screen.*

She brings about the universe by the power of her own free will, and not by any extraneous cause. The universe is already contained in her implicitly, and she makes it explicit.

Sūtra 3 : *This (i.e. the Universe) is manifold because of the differentiation of reciprocally adapted objects and subjects.*

The universe appears to be different and manifold because of the differentiation of experients and the objects experienced. These may be summarised thus :

1. At the level of *Sadāśiva-tattva*, the I-consciousness is more prominent; the experience of the universe is just in an incipient stage. The individual experient who rises to such a level of consciousness is known as Mantra-maheśvara and is directed by Sadāśiva. He has realized *Sadāśiva-tattva* and his experience is of the form — "I am this". The consciousness of this (the universe) is not fully marked out from the 'I' at this level.

2. At the level of *Īśvara-tattva*, the consciousness of both 'I' and 'this' is equally distinct. The individual experient who rises to this level is known as Mantreśvara. The universe is clearly distinct at this stage, but it is identified with the Self. Mantreśvara is directed by Īśvara.

3. At the level of *Vidyā-tattva*, the universe appears as different from 'I'. There is an experience of diversity, though there is unity in diversity. The individual experients of this stage are known as Mantras. They are directed by Ananta-bhaṭṭāraka. They have an experience of diversity all round, of the universe as being distinct from the Self (though it may still belong to the Self).

4. The stage of the experient below *Śuddha vidyā*, but above *Māyā* is that of *Vijñānākala*. His field of experience consists of *sakalas* and *pralayākalas*. He feels a sense of identity with them.

5. At the stage of Māyā, the experient is known as *pralayakevalin*. He has neither a clear consciousness of 'I', nor of 'this', and so his consciousness is practically that of the void.

6. From Māyā down to the earth, the experient is *sakala* who experiences diversity all round. The average human being belongs to this level.

Śiva transcends all manifestation. His experience is that of permanent bliss and identity with every thing from Sadāśiva down to the earth. Actually it is Śiva who flashes forth in various forms of manifestation.

Sūtra 4 : *The individual (experient) also, in whom citi or consciousness is contracted has the universe (as his body) in a contracted form.*

It is Śiva or Cit that by assuming contraction becomes both the universe and the experients of the universe.

Knowledge of this constitutes liberation.

Sūtra 5 : *Citi (universal consciousness) itself descending from (the stage of) Cetana becomes citta (individual consciousness) inasmuch as it becomes contracted in conformity with the object of consciousness.*

The universal consciousness itself becomes the individual consciousness by limitation.

The universal consciousness in the process of limitation has either (1) the predominance of *cit* or (2) the predominance of limitation.

In the former case, there is the stage of Vjñānākala when *prakāśa* is predominant, or Śuddha-vidyā-pramātā, when both *prakāśa* and *vimarśa* are predominant, or Īśa, Sadāśīva, Anāśrita-Śiva. In the latter case, there is the stage of Śūnya-pramātā etc.

The universal consciousness itself by assuming limitation becomes individual consciousness. Jñāna, Kriyā and Māyā of the universal consciousness become *sattva, rajas* and *tamas* in the case of the individual.

Sūtra 6 : The *māyā-pramātā* consists of it (i. e. *citta*).

The *māyā-pramātā* also is only Citta.

Sūtra 7 : *And (though) he is one, he becomes of two-fold form, three-fold, four-fold and of the nature of seven pentads.*

The *Cit* is Śiva Himself. Consciousness cannot be sundered by space and time.

Since by limitation it assumes the state of the experient and the object experienced, it is also of two forms. It also becomes three fold as it is covered with the *mala* pertaining to *aṇu, māyā,* and *karma*. It is also four fold, because it assumes the nature of (1) *śūnya*, (2) *prāṇa*, (3) *puryaṣṭaka*, and (4) the gross body. The seven pentads i.e. the thirtyfive *tattvas* below Śiva down to the earth is also its nature. From Śiva down to Sakala he also becomes seven fold experients and of the nature of five fold coverings (from Kalā to Niyati).

Sūtra 8 : *The positions of the various systems of philosophy are only various roles of that (consciousness or Self).*

The positions of the various systems of philosophy are, so to speak, roles assumed by the Self.

1. The Cārvākas, for instance, maintain that the Self is identical with the BODY characterised by consciousness.
2. The followers of Nyāya practically consider BUDDHI to be the Self in the worldly condition. After liberation, they consider Self as identical with the void.
3. The Mīmāṁsakas also practically consider Buddhi to be the Self inasmuch as they believe the I-CONSCIOUSNESS to be the Self.
4. The Buddhists also consider only the functions of BUDDHI as the Self.
5. Some Vedāntins regard PRĀṆA as the Self.
6. Some of the Vedāntins and the Mādhyamikas regard 'NON-BEING' as the fundamental principle.
7. The followers of Pāñcarātra believe Vāsudeva to be the highest cause.
8. The followers of Sāṅkhya practically accept the position of the Vijñānākalas.
9. Some Vedāntins accept ĪŚVARA as the highest principle.
10. The Grammarians consider PAŚYANTĪ or SADĀŚIVA to be the highest reality.
11. The Tāntrikas consider the ĀTMAN as transcending the universe to be the highest principle.
12. The Kaulas consider the UNIVERSE as the Ātman principle.
13. The followers of Trika philosophy maintain that the ĀTMAN is both immanent and transcendent.

The Sūtra may be interpreted in another way, viz., the experience of external things as colour etc., and internal experience as pleasure etc. become a means of the manifestation of the essential nature of Śiva or the highest reality.

Sūtra 9 : *In consequence of its limitation of Śakti, Reality which is all consciousness becomes the mala-covered saṁsārin.*

The Will-power being limited, there arises the *āṇava mala*, the *mala* pertaining to the *jīva* by which he considers himself to be imperfect.

Omniscience being limited, there arises knowledge of a few things only. Thus there comes to be *māyīya mala*, which consists in the apprehension of all objects as different.

Omnipotence being limited, the *jīva* acquires *kārma mala*.

Thus due to limitation, *sarva-kartṛtva* (Omnipotence) becomes *kalā* (limited agency), *sarvajñatva* (Omniscience) becomes *vidyā* (limitation in respect of knowledge), *pūrṇatva* (all fulfilment) becomes *rāga* (limitation in respect of desire), *nityatva* (eternity) becomes *Kāla* (limitation in respect of time), *vyāpakatva* (Omnipresence) becomes *niyati* (limitation in respect of space and cause). Jīva (the individual soul) is this limited self. When his Śakti is unfolded, he becomes Śiva Himself.

Sūtra 10 : *Even in this condition (of empirical self), he (the individual soul) does the five kṛtyas like Him (i.e. like Śiva).*

Just as Śiva does the five fold act in mundane manifestation as an unfoldment of His real nature, so does He do it—in the limited condition of a *jīva*.

The appearance of objects in a definite space and time is tantamount to *sraṣṭṛtā* (emanation), their appearance in another space and time and thus their disappearance to the individual soul constitutes *saṁhartṛtā* (withdrawal); continuity of the appearance of the objects constitutes *sthāpakatā* (maintenance). Because of the appearance of difference, there is *vilaya* (concealment).

When the object is identical with the light of consciousness, it is *anugraha* (grace).

Sūtra 11 : *He also does the five-fold act of manifesting, relishing, thinking out, setting of the seed and dissolution.* This is so from the esoteric stand-point of the Yogin.

Whatever is perceived is *ābhāsana* or *sṛṣṭi*. The perception is relished for sometime. This is *rakti* or *sthiti*. It is withdrawn at the time of knowledge. This is *saṁhāra*.

If the object of experience generates impressions of doubt etc., it becomes in germ the cause of transmigratory existence. This is *bījāvasthāpana* or *vilaya*.

If the object of experience is identified with consciousness, it is the state of *vilāpana* or *anugraha*.

Sūtra 12 : *To be a saṁsārin means being deluded by one's own powers because of the ignorance of that (i.e. authorship of the five-fold act.)*

In the absence of the knowledge of the five-fold act, one becomes deluded by one's own powers, and thus transmigrates ever and anon.

While talking of *śakti*, we would do well to realize that the highest Vāk śakti has the knowledge of the perfect 'I'. She is the great *mantra* inclusive of the letters 'a' to kṣa', and revealing the empirical experient. At this stage, she conceals the pure distinctionless consciousness and throws up ever new forms different from one another.

The empirical experient deluded by the various powers considers the body, prāṇa etc. as the Self. Brāhmī and other *śaktis* bring about emanation and maintenance of difference and withdrawal of identity in the empirical subject (*paśudaśā*).

At the stage of '*pati*', they do the reverse i.e. bring about the emanation and maintenance of identity, and withdrawal of difference. Gradually they bring about the state of '*avikalpa*'. This is known as pure Vikalpa power.

The above technique of establishing unity-consciousness is known as '*Śāmbhavopāya*'.

Now follows *Śāktopāya* or *Śākta* technique of unity — Consciousness.

Cit-śakti in this context is known as *Vāmeśvarī*. Her sub-species are *khecarī*, *gocarī*, *dikcarī*, *bhūcarī*. These bring about objectification of the universal consciousness. By *khecarī śakti*, the universal consciousness becomes an individual subject; by *gocarī śakti*, he becomes endowed with an inner psychic apparatus; by *dikcarī śakti*, he is endowed with outer senses, by *bhūcarī*, he is confined to external objects. By yogic practice, *khecarī* brings about consciousness of perfect agency; *gocarī* brings about consciousness of non-difference, *dikcarī* brings about a sense of non-difference in perception, *bhūcarī* brings about a consciousness of all objects as parts of one Self.

There is a third technique known as *āṇavopāya*. When the *aiśvarya śakti* of the Lord conceals her real nature in the case of the individual and deludes him by *prāṇa* etc., by the various states of waking, dreaming etc, and by the body both gross and subtle, he becomes a *saṁsārin*. When in the yogic process, she unfolds the *udāna śakti*, and the *vyāna śakti*, the individual comes to acquire the experience of *turya* and *turyātīta* states, and becomes liberated while living.

Sūtra 13 : *Acquiring full knowledge of it (i.e. of the five-fold act of the Self) Citta itself becomes Citi by rising to the status of cetana.*

When the knowledge of the five-fold act of the Self dawns on the individual, ignorance is removed. The *Citta* (individual consciousness) is no longer deluded by its own limiting powers; it re-captures its original freedom, and by acquiring a knowledge of its real nature, rises to the status of *Citi* (i.e. universal consciousness).

Sūtra 14 : *The fire of Citi even when it descends to the (lower) stage, though covered (by māyā) partly burns the fuel of the known (i.e. the objects).*

If *citi* is non-differentiating consciousness intrinsically, why is it that it is characterized by a sense of difference at the level of the individual ?

The answer is that even at the level of the individual, *Citi* does not completely lose its nature of non-differentiation, for all the multifarious objects as known are assimilated to *Citi* itself i.e. in the knowledge-situation, the objects become a part and parcel of *Citi*. As fire reduces to itself every thing thrown into it, even so, *Citi* assimilates to itself all the objects of knowledge. Only owing to its being covered by *Māyā*, *citi* does not reduce objects of knowledge to itself completely, for owing to the previous impressions (*saṁskāras*),), these objects appear again.

Sūtra 15 : *In the re-assertion of its (inherent) power, it makes the universe its own.*

Bala or power means the emergence of the real nature of *Citi*. Then *Citi* manifests the whole universe as identical with itself. This is not the temporary play of Citi, it is rather its permanent nature. It is always inclusive, for without this inclusive nature of *Citi* even body and other objects would not be known. Therefore, the practice recommended for acquiring the power of *Citi* is meant only for the removal of the false identification of oneself with the body etc.

Sūtra 16 : *When the bliss of Cit is attained, there is the lasting acquisition of that state in which Cit is our only Self, and in which all things that appear are identical with Cit. Even the body etc. that is experienced appears as identical with Cit.*

The steady experience of identity with *Cit* means *jīvanmukti* (liberation even in this physical body). This comes about by the dissolution of ignorance on the recognition of one's true nature.

Sūtra 17 : *By the development of the centre is acquisition of the bliss of the spirit.*

By the development of the centre can the bliss of the spirit be obtained. *Saṁvit* or the power of consciousness is called the centre, because it is the support or ground of every thing in the world. In the individual, it is symbolized by the central *nāḍī* i.e. *suṣumnā*. When the central consciousness in man develops or when the *suṣumnā nāḍī* develops, then is there the bliss of the universal consciousness.

Sūtra 18 : *Herein (i.e. for the development of the Centre) the means are :*

Dissolution of vikalpa; saṅkoca-vikāsa of Śakti; cutting of the vāhas; the practice (of the contemplation) of the koṭi (point) of the beginning and the end.

The first method is *vikalpakṣaya*. One should concentrate on the heart, should not allow any *vikalpa* to arise, and thus by reducing the mind to an *avikalpa* condition, and holding the Self as the real experient in the focus of consciousness, one would develop the *madhya* or consciousness of central reality and would enter the *turya* and *turyātīta* condition. This is the main method of Pratyabhijñā for *madhya-vikāsa*.

The other methods do not belong to Pratyabhijñā but are recommended for their utility. *Saṅkoca* and *vikāsa of śakti*. *Saṅkoca* of *śakti* means withdrawing of consciousness that rushes out through the gates of the senses, and turning it inwardly towards the Self. *Vikāsa* of *śakti* means holding the consciousness steadily within, while the senses are allowed to perceive their objects. Another way of acquiring *saṅkoca* and *vikāsa* of *śakti* is the practice of *prasara* and *viśrānti* in the stage of *ūrdhva kuṇḍalinī*. Emergence from *samādhi* while retaining its experience is *prasara or vikāsa*, and merging back into *samādhi* and resting in that condition is *viśrānti or saṅkoca*.

A third method is *vāha-ccheda* i.e. cessation of *prāṇa* and *apāna* by repeating inwardly the letters 'ka', 'ha' etc. without the vowels, and tracing the *mantras* back to their source where they are unuttered.

A fourth method is *ādyanta-koṭi-nibhālana* i.e. the practice of fixing the mind at the time of the arising of *prāṇa* and its coming to an end between the *ādi* i.e. the first or heart and the *anta* i.e. the distance of twelve fingers from the point between the two eye-brows.

Sūtra 19 : ***In vyutthāna which is full of the after-effects of samādhi, there is the attainment of permanent samādhi, by dwelling on one's identity with Cit (universal consciousness) over and over again.***

Even on the occasion of *vyutthāna*, the yogin sees the entire universe dissolve in *Cit* by the process of *nimīlana-samādhi*. Thus he acquires permanent *samādhi* by *Krama-mudrā*.

Sūtra 20 : *Then (i.e. on the attainment of Kramamudrā), as a result of entering into the perfect I-consciousness or Self which, is in essence cit and ānanda (i.e. consciousness and bliss) and of the nature of the great mantra-power, there accrues the attainment of lordship over one's group of the deities of consciousness that bring about all emanation and re-absorption of the universe. All this is the nature of Śiva.*

When one masters *kramamudrā* etc., one enters into the real perfect I-consciousness or Self, and acquires mastery or lordship over the group of consciousness-deities that bring about emanation and absorption of the universe. The perfect I-consciousness is full of light and bliss. No longer is the individual deluded into considering his body, gross or subtle, *prāṇa* or senses as the 'I', he now considers the divine light within as the real 'I'. This real 'I' is the *saṁvit, sadāśiva* and *Maheśvara.* This I-consciousness means the resting of all objective experience within the Self. It is also called *Svātantrya* or sovereignty of Will, the primary agency of everything and lordship. This consciousness of pure 'I' is the *fons et origo* of all the *mantras,* and therefore it is of great power. It is the universal *Cit* itself. By acquiring this consciousness, one becomes the master of these *śaktis* that bring about the emanation and absorption of the universe.

ओं नमो मङ्गलमूर्तये ।

अथ

प्रत्यभिज्ञाहृदयम् ।

नमः शिवाय सततं पञ्चकृत्यविधायिने ।
चिदानन्दघनस्वात्मपरमार्थावभासिने ॥ १ ॥
शांकरोपनिषत्सारप्रत्यभिज्ञामहोदधेः ।
क्षेमेणोद्ध्रियते सारः संसारविषशान्तये ॥ २ ॥

OM — Adoration to one who is the very embodiment of bliss and auspiciousness

NOW (commences)

THE PRATYABHIJÑĀHṚDAYA

[The Secret of Recognition[1]]

Adoration to Śiva[2] who eternally[3] brings about the five processes,[4] who makes manifest the Highest Reality which is at the same time the Highest Value[5] viz., His Self[6] (which is also the Real Self of each individual) that is a mass of consciousness and bliss.[7]

Out of the great ocean (of the doctrine) of Recognition which is the quintessence of the secret doctrine[8] concerning Śaṁkara[9] is brought out the cream (i.e. the essential part) by Kṣemarāja to nullify the poison of *saṁsāra*.[10]

इह ये सुकुमारमतयोऽकृततीक्ष्णतर्कशास्त्रपरिश्रमाः शक्तिपातोन्मिषित-पारमेश्वरसमावेशाभिलाषिणः कतिचित् भक्तिभाजः तेषाम् ईश्वरप्रत्यभिज्ञो-पदेशतत्त्वं मनाक् उन्मील्यते ।

तत्र स्वात्मदेवताया एव सर्वत्र कारणत्वं सुखोपायप्राप्यत्वं महाफलत्वं च अभिव्यङ्क्तुमाह—

चितिः स्वतन्त्रा विश्वसिद्धिहेतुः ॥ १ ॥

'विश्वस्य' – सदाशिवादेः भूम्यन्तस्य 'सिद्धौ'–निष्पत्तौ, प्रकाशने, स्थित्यात्मनि, परप्रमातृविश्रान्त्यात्मनि च संहारे, पराशक्तिरूपा 'चितिः' भगवती

In this world, there are some devoted people, who are undeveloped in reflection and have not taken pains in studying difficult works like Logic and Dialectics, but who nevertheless aspire after *Samāveśa*[11] with the highest Lord which blossoms forth with the descent of Śakti.[12] For their sake, the truth of the teaching of *Īśvara-pratyabhijñā** is being explained briefly.

In order to explain the universal causality of the divinity that is the Self (of all), its attainability by easy means, and the high reward, it is said (lit., he says) :

Sutra 1.[13] The absolute[14] Citi[15] of its own free will is the cause of the Siddhi[16] of the universe.

Commentary

'Of the universe or *Viśva*' means from Sadāśiva[17] etc. down to the earth. (In the matter of) *Siddhi* means 'in effectuation' i.e., in bringing about *sṛṣṭi* or manifestation, *sthiti* or continued existence, and *saṁhāra* or resting in the Highest Experient.[18] (In bringing about all this), the Highest Śakti,[19] viz. the

---

* This is a great and well-reasoned out work on Pratyabhijñā by Utpalācārya who flourished in the 9th century A.D. Prof. Leidecker translates even Īśvara-pratyabhijñā. He is unable to see that what Kṣemarāja means to say is that he is giving a summary of the teachings of Īśvarapratyabhijñā.

'स्वतन्त्रा' – अनुत्तरविमर्शमयी शिवभट्टारकाभिन्ना 'हेतुः' – कारणम् । अस्यां हि प्रसरन्त्यां जगत् उन्मिषति व्यवतिष्ठते च, निवृत्तप्रसरायां च निःमिषति; –इति स्वानुभव एव अत्र साक्षी । अन्यस्य तु मायाप्रकृत्यादेः चित्प्रकाशभिन्नस्य अप्रकाशमानत्वेन असत्त्वात् न क्वचिदपि हेतुत्वम्; प्रकाशमानत्वे तु प्रकाशैकात्म्यात् प्रकाशरूपा चितिरेव हेतुः; न त्वसौ कश्चित् । अत एव देशकालाकारा एतत्सृष्टा एतदनुप्राणिताश्च नैतत्स्वरूपं भेत्तुमलम्; – इति व्यापक-नित्योदित-परिपूर्णरूपा इयम्-इत्यर्थलभ्यमेव एतत् ।

divine consciousness—power which is absolute and of free will, consists of the highest *vimarśa*,[20*] and is non-distinct from *Śivabhaṭṭārka*[21] is the *hetu* or cause. It is only when *Citi*, the ultimate consciousness—power, comes into play that the universe comes forth into being (lit. opens its eyelids), and continues as existent, and when it withdraws its movement, the universe also disappears from view (lit. shuts its eye lids). One's own experience would bear witness to this fact (lit. in this matter). The other things, viz., *Māyā*, *Prakṛti* etc., since they are (supposed to be) different from the light of consciousness can never be a cause of anything (lit. anywhere), for not being able to appear owing to their supposed difference from consciousness-power, they are (as good as) non-existent. But if they appear, they become one with the light (of consciousness). Hence *Citi* which is that light alone is the cause. Never is the other one (viz., *Māyā*, *Prakṛti*) any cause. Therefore, space, time, and form which have been brought into being and are vitalized by it (*Citi*) are not capable of penetrating its real nature, because it is all-pervading, eternal (lit. ever risen),[22] and completely full (in itself). This is to be understood by the import (of the *Sūtra*).

---

* *Vimarśa* is a highly technical term of this system. See note no. 20. Prof. Leidecker translates it as 'reason' (which is the dictionary meaning). This is entirely erroneous. It is not reason which brings about this world, nor is it absolute and of free will.

ननु जगदपि चितो भिन्नं नैव किञ्चित्; अभेदे च कथं हेतुहेतुमद्भावः? उच्यते। चिदेव भगवती स्वच्छस्वतन्त्ररूपा तत्तदनन्तजगदात्मना स्फुरति,– इत्येतावत्परमार्थोऽयं कार्यकारणभावः। यतश्च इयमेव प्रमातृ-प्रमाण-प्रमेय-मयस्य विश्वस्य सिद्धौ–प्रकाशने हेतुः, ततोऽस्याः स्वतन्त्रापरिच्छिन्नस्वप्रकाश-रूपायाः सिद्धौ अभिनवार्थप्रकाशनरूपं न प्रमाणवराकमुपयुक्तम् उपपन्नं वा। तदुक्तं त्रिकसारे—

It may be objected. (If all is *cit* or consciousness then), is not the universe itself non-existent (lit. nothing whatsoever), different as it is from *Cit* (consciousness)? If it be maintained that the universe is non-different (from *Cit*), how can one establish the relation of cause and its effect (between *cit* and *jagat* if they are identical).*

The answer is — It is the divine consciousness alone (*cideva bhagavatī*) — luminous, absolute and free-willed as it is, which flashes forth in the form of innumerable worlds. This is what is meant by the causal relation here. It is used in its highest sense.§ Since this (i.e. consciousness) alone is the cause of the *Siddhi* i.e. manifestation of the universe which consists of *pramātṛ*[23] (subjects or knowers), *pramāṇa*[24] (knowledge and its means), and *prameya*[25] (objects or the known), therefore poor means of proof (*pramāṇa*) whose main function is to bring to light new objects, is neither fit nor qualified to prove the (ultimate) consciousness, (which is ever present) which is absolute, unlimited and self-luminous. This is declared in *Trikasāra* (as follows):

---

*i.e. In causal relation, the effect is believed to be different from the cause. *Cit* is supposed to be the cause of the universe, but if the universe is non-different from the cause, how can it be its effect? (for the effect must be different from the cause).

§ In the highest sense, the causal relation does not mean succession, but simultaneous expression. The flutter of *Citi* is simultaneous manifestation of the universe.

'स्वपदा स्वशिरश्छायां यद्वल्लङ्घितुमीहते ।
पादोद्देशे शिरो न स्यात्तथेयं बैन्दवी कला ।।'

इति ।

यतश्च इयं विश्वस्य सिद्धौ पराद्वयसामरस्यापादनात्मनि च संहारे हेतुः, तत एव स्वतन्त्रा । प्रत्यभिज्ञातस्वातन्त्र्या सती, भोगमोक्षस्वरूपाणां विश्वसिद्धीनां हेतुः ।—इति आवृत्त्या व्याख्येयम् ।

अपि च 'विश्वं'—नील—सुख—देह—प्राणादि; तस्य या 'सिद्धिः'—प्रमाणोपारोहक्रमेण विमर्शमयप्रमात्रावेशः, सैव 'हेतुः'—परिज्ञाने उपायो यस्याः । अनेन

Just as (when) one tries to jump over the shadow of one's head with one's own foot, the head will never be at the place of one's foot, so (also) is it with *baindavī Kalā*.[26]

Since it (consciousness) is the cause of the *siddhi* of the universe—as well as *saṁhāra* which consists in bringing about—*sāmarasya*[27] or identity with the highest non-dual (consciousness), therefore is it called *svatantrā*[28] i.e. free-willed. Its free will being recognized, it becomes the cause of the *siddhi** (i.e. attainment) of the universe, which *siddhi* is of the nature of *bhoga* i.e. experience and *mokṣa* i.e. [29]liberation (from the bondage of limited experience). By repetition, the *sūtra* should be interpreted in the above sense also.

[Now the word 'hetu' is taken in the sense of means.] Again, *viśva* or universe means (external objects like) blue (etc.), (internal feeling like) pleasure, (limited experient) body, *prāṇa* etc. Its (i.e. of the *Viśva*) *siddhi* (i.e., fulfilment or establishment) is the *hetu* or means of the awareness of *Citi*. This *siddhi* consists in the *āveśa* or merging in the Self which is of the nature of *vimarśa* by gradual mounting, beginning with *pramāṇa* or knowledge[30] (and coming to rest in the *pramātā* or

* *Siddhi* also means fruition, attainment, perfection. It is in this sense that the writer now interprets the word '*Siddhi*'.

च सुखोपायत्वमुक्तम् । यदुक्तं श्रीविज्ञानभट्टारके—

'ग्राह्यग्राहकसंवित्तिः सामान्या सर्वदेहिनाम् ।
योगिनां तु विशेषोऽयं संबन्धे सावधानता ॥'

इति ।

'चितिः'—इति एकवचनं देशकालाद्यनवच्छिन्नताम् अभिदधत् समस्तभेदवादानाम् अवास्तवतां व्यनक्ति । 'स्वतन्त्र'-शब्दो ब्रह्मवादवैलक्षण्यम् आचक्षाणः चितो माहेश्वर्यसारतां ब्रूते । 'विश्व'—इत्यादिपदम् अशेषशक्तित्वं, सर्वकारणत्वं, सुखोपायत्वं महाफलं च आह ॥ १ ॥

knower). By 'means' is meant here 'easy means'.† As is said in the excellent *Vijñānabhaṭṭāraka* (*Vijñānabhairava*, v. 106) :

"The consciousness of object and subject is common to all the embodied ones. The *Yogins*, however, have this distinction that they are mindful of this relation" (i.e. the object is always related to the subject; without this relation to the subject there is no such thing as an object. The yogī is always conscious of that witnessing awareness from which the subject arises and in which it finally rests).

Citi (consciousness) used in the singular (in the *sūtra*) denotes its non-limitation by space, time etc., (and thus), shows the unreality of all theories of dualism. The word *svatantra* (absolute, of free will) (in the *sūtra*) points out the fact that supreme power is of the essence of *cit*, and thus distinguishes it from the doctrine of Brahman[31] (i.e. Śaṅkara Vedānta, where the *Cit* is considered to be non-active). The word *viśva* etc. declares that it (*Cit*) has unlimited power, can bring about every thing, is an easy means (for emancipation), and is the great reward (i.e. it is an end in itself).

† '*Sukhopāya*' does not mean 'way to happiness' as Prof. Leidecker thinks.

ननु विश्वस्य यदि चितिः हेतुः, तत् अस्या उपादानाद्यपेक्षायां भेदवादा-परित्यागः स्यात्–इत्याशङ्क्य आह—

स्वेच्छया स्वभित्तौ विश्वमुन्मीलयति ॥ २ ॥

'स्वेच्छया', न तु ब्रह्मादिवत् अन्येच्छया, तयैव च, न तु उपादानाद्यपेक्षया,– एवं हि प्रागुक्तस्वातन्त्र्यहान्या चित्त्वमेव न घटेत–'स्वभित्तौ', न तु अन्यत्र क्वापि, प्राक् निर्णीतं 'विश्वं' दर्पणे नगरवत् अभिन्नमपि भिन्नमिव 'उन्मीलयति'।

But here a question arises—If *Citi* is the cause of the universe, it would presuppose material cause etc., (in order to bring about this apparently different universe) and (thus there would be) non-abandonment of dualism. Apprehending this (question), he (the author) says :

Sūtra 2. By the power of her own will (alone), she (citi) unfolds the universe upon her own screen (i.e. in herself as the basis of the universe).

Commentary

Svecchayā—i.e. by the power of her own will, not by the will of another as (is maintained by) the Brahman doctrine, and similar (systems). Moreover (the phrase) 'by the power of her own will' implies (that she brings about the universe) by her power *alone*, not by means of (any extraneous) material cause etc. In this way (i.e. on the presupposition of material cause etc.), if the aforesaid absolute, free will is denied to her (i.e. to *Citi*), her *Cit*-ness itself would not be possible (i.e. *Cit* and free will are inseparable).

Svabhittau means on her own screen (i.e. in herself as the basis), not anywhere else. She unfolds the previously defined universe (i.e. from Sadāśiva down to the earth) like a city

उन्मीलनं च अवस्थितस्यैव प्रकटीकरणम् ।—इत्यनेन जगतः प्रकाशैकात्म्येन अवस्थानम् उक्तम् ॥ २ ॥

अथ विश्वस्य स्वरूपं विभागेन प्रतिपादयितुमाह—

तन्नाना अनुरूपग्राह्यग्राहकभेदात् ॥ ३ ॥

'तत्' विश्वं 'नाना' —अनेकप्रकारम् । कथं ? 'अनुरूपाणां'— परस्परौचित्यावस्थितीनां 'ग्राह्याणां ग्राहकाणां' च 'भेदात्' —वैचित्र्यात् । तथा च सदाशिवतत्त्वे अहन्ताच्छादित-अस्फुटेदन्तामयं यादृशं परापररूपं विश्वं ग्राह्यं, तादृगेव श्रीसदाशिवभट्टारकाधिष्ठितो मन्त्रमहेश्वराख्यः प्रमातृवर्गः परमेश्वरेच्छाव-

in a mirror, which though non-different from it appears as different.[32] *Unmilana* means only making explicit what is already lying (implicit) (in *citi*). By this is meant the existence of the universe (in *citi*) as identical with the light (of *citi*).

Now in order to make clear the nature of the universe by means of analysis, he (the author) says :—

Sūtra 3. That (i.e. the universe) is manifold because of the differentiation of reciprocally adapted (anurūpa) objects (grāhya) and subjects (grāhaka).

Commentary

Tat (that) means the universe; '*nānā*' means manifold. Why (manifold) ? Because of the differentiation (*bheda*) between objects and subjects which are *anurūpa* i.e. in a state of reciprocal adaptation.

[The correspondence or reciprocal adaptation of object and subject now follows].

Just as in the *Sadāśiva* principle, (there is the experience of) the total universe (*Viśva*) as an object (*grāhya*) of the

कल्पिततथावस्थानः । ईश्वरतत्त्वे स्फुटेदन्ताहन्तासामानाधिकरण्यात्म यादृक् विश्वं ग्राह्यं, तथाविध एव ईश्वरभट्टारकाधिष्ठितो मन्त्रेश्वरवर्गः । विद्यापदे श्रीमदनन्तभट्टारकाधिष्ठिता बहुशाखावान्तरभेदभिन्ना यथाभूता मन्त्राः प्रमातारः, तथाभूतमेव भेदैकसारं विश्वमपि प्रमेयम् । मायोर्ध्वे यादृशा विज्ञानाकलाः कर्तृताशून्यशुद्धबोधात्मानः, तादृगेव तदभेदसारं सकल-प्रलयाकलात्मक-पूर्वावस्था-परिचितम् एषां प्रमेयम् । मायायां शून्यप्रमातॄणां प्रलयकेवलिनां स्वोचितं प्रलीनकल्पं प्रमेयम् । क्षितिपर्यन्तावस्थितानां तु सकलानां सर्वतो भिन्नानां

nature of *parā-para* i.e. both identical and different, (a stage in which the experience is of the form 'I am this') (in which) the experience is dominated (*ācchādita*) by the Consciousness of I (*ahantā*), and (in which the experience of) this-ness (*idantā*) is (yet) incipient (*asphuṭa*), even so there is the group of experients (*pramātārs*), called *mantramaheśvaras* who are governed by the blessed Lord Sadāśiva,[33] and whose existence in that state is brought about by the will of the highest Lord.

Just as in the *Īśvara tattva* (principle), the entire universe is apprehended (*grāhya*) (in the form, "I am this") where both the consciousness of I (*ahantā*) and that of this (*idantā*) are simultaneously distinct (*sphuṭa*), even so (*tathāvidha eva*) is (the consciousness of) the group of individual experients, (known as) *mantreśvara*, governed by venerable Īśvara.[34]

In the stage of Vidyā or Śuddha Vidyā, just as there are the experients, called Mantras, of different states together with many secondary distinctions, governed by Anantabhaṭṭāraka, even so there is as an object of knowledge (*prameya*) one universe whose sole essence consists of differentiations.[35]

Above Māyā (and below Śuddha Vidyā) are the experients, called Vijñānākalas who are devoid of (the sense of) agency (*kartṛtā*), and who are of the nature of pure awareness (*Śuddha-bodhātmānaḥ*). Corresponding to them is their object

परिमितानां तथाभूतमेव प्रमेयम् । तदुत्तीर्णशिवभट्टारकस्य प्रकाशैकवपुषः प्रकाशैक-रूपा एव भावाः । श्रीमत्परमशिवस्य पुनः विश्वोत्तीर्ण-विश्वात्मक-परमानन्दमय-प्रकाशैकघनस्य एवंविधमेव शिवादि-धरण्यन्तम् अखिलम अभेदेनैव स्फुरति; न तु वस्तुतः अन्यत् किंचित् ग्राह्यं ग्राहकं वा; अपि तु श्रीपरमशिवभट्टारक एव इत्थं नानावैचित्र्यसहस्रैः स्फुरति ।–इत्यभिहितप्रायम् ॥ ३ ॥

यथा च भगवान् विश्वशरीरः, तथा

of knowledge or field of experience (*prameya*) which is identical with them (*tadabhedasāram*) (consisting of) *sakalas* and *pralayākalas* known to them (*paricita*) in their previous states of existence (*pūrvāvasthā*).[36]

At the stage of Māyā, (are) the experients of void (*Śūnya*) or *pralayakevalins* whose field of experiencs practically consists of the insensible which is quite appropriate to their state.[37]

(After the *pralayākalas*) are stationed the *sakalas* (from Māyā) upto the earth who are different from every thing and limited, and whose field of experience is as limited and different as themselves (*tathābhūtam*).[38]

Śivabhaṭṭāraka, however, who transcends all these (i.e. all the experients from Mantramaheśvara to Sakala), who is constituted only of *prakāśa* (light) has states or modes which are only of the form of *prakāśa* (light i.e.. consciousness).[39] Again in blissful Paramaśiva (highest Śiva) who both transcends the universe and is the universe, who is highest bliss and consists of a mass of *prakāśa* (light i.e. consciousness) flashes the entire universe from Śiva down to the earth in identity (with Parama Śiva). Actually (in that state), there is neither any other subject (*grāhaka*) nor object (*grāhya*). Rather what is practically meant to be stated (*abhihitaprāyam*) is this that in actuality the highest blissful Śiva alone manifests himself in this way in numerous forms of multiplicity.

As the Lord has the entire universe as his body, so

चितिसंकोचात्मा चेतनोऽपि संकुचितविश्वमयः ॥ ४ ॥

श्रीपरमशिवः स्वात्मैक्येन स्थितं विश्वं सदाशिवाद्युचितेन रूपेण अवबिभासयिषुः पूर्वं चिदैक्याख्यातिमयानाश्रितशिवपर्यायशून्यातिशून्यात्मतया प्रकाशाभेदेन प्रकाशमानतया स्फुरति; ततः चिद्रसाश्यानतारूपाशेषतत्त्वभुवनभाव-

Sūtra 4. The (individual) experient also, in whom citi or consciousness is contracted has the universe (as his body) in a contracted form.*

Commentary

The magnificent highest Śiva desiring to manifest the universe, which lies in Him as identical with Himself, in the form of Sadāśiva and other appropriate forms flashes forth (*prakāśamānatayā sphurati*) at first as non-different from the light (of consciousness) (*prakāśābhedena*) but not experiencing the unity of consciousness (in which the universe is identified with consciousness) (*cidaikya-akhyātimaya*),§ of which state *anāśrita-śiva* is only another name, (*anāśrita-Śiva-paryāya*),[40] and being (as yet) more void than the void itself (from the point of view of any objective manifestation).[41] Then He unfolds Himself in the totality of manifestations viz., principles (*tattvas*), worlds (*bhuvanas*), entities (*bhāvas*) and their respective experients (*pramātāras*) that are only a solidified form (*āśyānatārūpa*) of Cit-essence.‡

---

* Prof. Leidecker translates it in the following way: "has cetana, which is qualified by the contraction of Citi, been formed of the contracted universe". This hardly makes any sense.

§ *Akhyāti* is that state which for the time being negates or keeps away from Śiva the consciousness of his full nature (*Śiva svarūpāpohanam*).

‡ Prof. Leidecker gives a curious translation of this sentence, viz "He is their true nature, when they distinguish themselves by not having lost the savour of cit". *Cit-rasa* does not mean 'the savour of cit,' but the essence of *cit*, and *āśyānatā* does not mean non-distinction, but solidification, i.e. concrete manifestation of the subtle essence of *cit* (*cit-rasa*). Rasa is sap or juice in this context, and suggests that as liquid juice may be solidified, even so *cit* may assume concrete manifestation.

तत्तत्प्रमातृप्राह्यात्मतयापि प्रथते । यथा च एवं भगवान् विश्वशरीरः, तथा 'चितिसंकोचात्मा' संकुचितचिद्रूपः; 'चेतनो' ग्राहकोऽपि वटधानिकावत् संकुचिताशेषविश्वरूपः । तथा च सिद्धान्तवचनम्

'विग्रहो विग्रही चैव सर्वविग्रहविग्रही ।'

इति । त्रिशिरोमतेऽपि

सर्वदेवमयः कायस्तं चेदानीं शृणु प्रिये ।
पृथिवी कठिनत्वेन द्रवत्वेऽम्भः प्रकीर्तितम् ॥'

इत्युपक्रम्य

'त्रिशिरोभैरवः साक्षाद्व्याप्य विश्वं व्यवस्थितः ॥'

इत्यन्तेन ग्रन्थेन ग्राहकस्य संकुचितविश्वमयत्वमेव व्याहरति ।

As thus the Lord is universe-bodied (*bhagavān viśvaśarīraḥ*) so the (individual) experient also, because of consciousness being contracted, has the body of the entire universe in a contracted form even as the *vaṭa* tree is in a contracted form in its seed. So does the Siddhānta (the settled doctrine of the system) say :

"One body and embodied really include all the bodies and the embodied."

Triśiromata[42] also declares that the subject or self becomes the universe in a contracted form. Beginning (thus) :

"The body is of the form of all gods;[43] hear now, concerning it, my dear.[44] It is called earth because of its solidity, and water because of its fluidity," it ends by saying.

"The three-headed Bhairava[45] is present in person (*sākṣāt vyavasthitaḥ*), pervading the entire universe."

अयं च अत्राशयः—ग्राहकोऽपि अयं प्रकाशैकात्म्येन उक्तागमयुक्त्या च विश्वशरीरशिवैकरूप एव, केवलं तन्मायाशक्त्या अनभिव्यक्तस्वरूपत्वात् संकुचित इव आभाति; संकोचोऽपि विचार्यमाणः चिदैकात्म्येन प्रथमानत्वात् चिन्मय एव, अन्यथा तु न किंचित् ।–इति सर्वो ग्राहको विश्वशरीरः शिवभट्टारक एव। तदुक्तं मयैव

'अख्यातिर्यदि न ख्याति ख्यातिरेवावशिष्यते।
ख्याति चेत् ख्यातिरूपत्वात् ख्यातिरेवावशिष्यते ॥'

इति। अनेनैव आशयेन श्रीस्पन्दशास्त्रेषु

'यस्मात्सर्वमयो जीवः ……।'

Here this is the implication. The experient or subject is identical with Śiva whose body is the universe, because light (of consciousness) is his true nature, and because of the reasonings of the Āgamas (just) mentioned; only because of his (Śiva's) *Māyā-Śakti* he (the experient) appears as contracted, because his real nature is not manifested. Contraction also, on (close) consideration, consists of *cit* (consciousness) only, since it is manifested only as of the nature of *cit*, otherwise (i.e. in the absence of its being manifested, and it can be manifested only when it is of the nature of consciousness), it becomes mere nothing. Thus every subject is identical with revered Śiva whose body is the universe. It has been said by myself (elsewhere).

"If it be said that *akhyāti* or nescience is that which never appears i.e. which is never experienced, then appearance, or knowledge alone remains. If it be said that *akhyāti* does appear i.e. is experienced (in some form), then (obviously) being of the nature of knowledge, knowledge alone remains.[46]

With this intention, the identity of the *Jiva* (the individual experient), and Śiva (the universal experient) has been declared in *Spandaśāstra*[47] (in the verse) starting with :

इत्युपक्रम्य

'तेन शब्दार्थचिन्तासु न सावस्था न यः शिवः ॥'

इत्यादिना शिवजीवयोरभेद एव उक्तः । एतत्तत्त्वपरिज्ञानमेव मुक्तिः, एतत्तत्त्वापरिज्ञानमेव च बन्धः; –इति भविष्यति एव एतत् ॥ ४ ॥

ननु ग्राहकोऽयं विकल्पमयः, विकल्पनं च चित्तहेतुकं; सति च चित्ते, कथमस्य शिवात्मकत्वम् ?–इति शङ्कित्वा चित्तमेव निर्णेतुमाह—

"Because the *Jiva* is identical with the whole universe", and concluding with (the line) "Hence whether in the word or object or mental apprehension there is no state which is not Śiva"* [*Spandakārikā* of Vasugupta — Niṣyanda, II. vv. 3-4.]

Knowledge of this truth alone constitutes liberation; want of the knowledge of this truth alone constitutes bondage. This will be surely cleared later on (lit., this will come to pass).

An objection might be raisedviz., the subject or experient is of the nature of *vikalpa*,[48] and *vikalpa* is due to *Citta*.[49] *Citta* being there (i.e. being the nature of the subject), how can he (the subject) be of the nature of Śiva.† Apprehending (such an objection), the (author) in order to settle (the connotation of) *Citta* itself, says:

*Prof. Leidecker gives peculiar translation of this "Therefore, if one reflects deeper on the meaning of the words, (one becomes aware that), this is not the condition, not the one that is Śiva." The last sentence— "this is not the condition......Śiva" is meaningless. Not being able to understand the meaning, he calls the text itself unintelligible in his note on p. 116. The text is not at all unintelligible. The simple meaning is "There is no state which is not Śiva". Another reading of the last half of this line is—'*na sāvasthā na yā Śivaḥ.*'

† What the objector means to say is this : The subject goes on making all kinds of *vikalpas*, for he does all his thinking by means of *citta*, and the nature of *citta* is to form *vikalpas*. So long as the *citta* lasts, how can the subject be of the nature of Siva who is *nirvikalpa*?

चितिरेव चेतनपदादवरूढा चेत्यसंकोचिनी चित्तम् ॥ ५ ॥

न चित्तं नाम अन्यत् किंचित्, अपि तु सैव भगवती तत् । तथा हि सा स्वं स्वरूपं गोपयित्वा यदा संकोचं गृह्णाति, तदा द्वयी गतिः; कदाचित् उल्लसितमपि संकोचं गुणीकृत्य चित्प्राधान्येन स्फुरति, कदाचित् संकोचप्रधानतया । चित्प्राधान्यपक्षे सहजे, प्रकाशमात्रप्रधानत्वे विज्ञानाकलता; प्रकाशपरामर्श-

Sūtra 5. "Citi (universal consciousness) itself descending from (the stage of) Cetana (the uncontracted conscious stage) becomes Citta (individual consciousness) inasmuch as it becomes contracted (Saṅkocinī) in conformity with the objects of consciousness (cetya)."

Commentary

Truly speaking *Citta* (individual consciousness) is not anything else, rather it is the exalted *Citi* (universal consciousness) itself. Now, when *Citi* concealing its real nature accepts contraction or limitation, then it has only two aspects. Sometimes it flashes forth with the predominance of *Cit*, subordinating to itself limitation which has made its appearance; sometimes (it appears) with the predominance of limitation In the case of *Cit* being predominant in its natural state, and there being the predominance of *prakāśa* only (without *vimarśa*), its *pramātṛ*, or experient is *Vijñānākala.*[50] In the case of both *prakāśa* and *vimarśa* being predominant,* the experient is *vidyāpramātā.*[51] Even in this state (*prakāśa-parāmarśa-*

---

*Prof. Leidecker has given a very curious translation of this, viz., "But when the (divine) light is being impaired". This neither conveys any sense; nor is it borne out by any linguistic or grammatical consideration. *Prakāśa-parāmarśa-pradhānatve* means 'in the case of *prakāśa* and *vimarśa* — both being predominant'. Here '*parāmarśa*' is a synonym of '*vimarśa*'.

प्रधानत्वे तु विद्याप्रमातृता । तत्रापि क्रमेण संकोचस्य तनुतायाम्, ईश-सदाशिवा-नाश्रितरूपता । समाधिप्रयत्नोपार्जिते तु चित्प्रधानत्वे शुद्धाध्वप्रमातृता क्रमात्क्रमं प्रकर्षवती । संकोचप्राधान्ये तु शून्यादिप्रमातृता । एवमवस्थिते सति, 'चितिरेव'

pradhānatve), as the contraction (of consciousness) is gradually less, there are the stages of Īśa, Sadāśiva and Anāśrita-Śiva.[52]§ In the predominance of *cit*, however, acquired through effort of contemplation (*samādhi*), the knowership of the pure path[53] reaches the highest degree by stages.‡

Where, however, contraction or limitation (of *cit*) is predominant, there occurs the knowership of the Void etc.[54]

This being the position, *citi* (the universal consciousness) itself, in the form of the limited subject, descending from its stage of *cetana* (universal consciousness), disposed towards comprehending objects, being limited by its objects of consciousness, like blue (i.e. external object of consciousness), pleasure (i.e. internal object of consciousness) etc. being limited by

---

§ Prof. Leidecker has translated '*tanutāyām* as corporeality'. This is simply absurd. The text, very clearly says, *Saṅkocasya tanutāyām Īśa-sadāśiva-anāśrita-rūpatā* i.e. in the case of the *tanutā* of contraction, there are the states of Īśa, Sadāśiva and Anāśrita-Śiva. If *tanutā* is to be translated as corporeality, as Prof. Leidecker has done, it would mean that the states of Īśa, Sadāśiva etc. get more and more corporeal. This would be the height of absurdity. *Tanutā* here means attenuation not corporeality.

‡ The idea is that *Cit-pradhānatva* (predominance of *cit*) is either natural (*sahaja*) or acquired through the effort of Samādhi (*Samādhi-prayatnopārjita*). In the predominance of *cit* which is of the natural type, there may be either predominance of *prakāśa* only in which case, the experient is Vijñānākala or there may be predominance of both *prakāśa* and *vimarśa* in which case the experients are the *Vidyāpramātaras*.

In the case of predominance of *Cit* acquired through the effort of Samādhi, the *Śuddhādhvapramātāras* reach the highest degree by stages

संकुचितग्राहकरूपा 'चेतनपदात् अवरूढा'—अर्थग्रहणोन्मुखी सती 'चेत्येन'—नील-सुखादिना 'संकोचिनी' उभयसंकोचसंकुचितैव चित्तम् । तथा च—

'स्वाङ्गरूपेषु भावेषु पत्युर्ज्ञानं क्रिया च या ।
मायातृतीये ते एव पशोः सत्वं रजस्तमः ॥'

इत्यादिना स्वातन्त्र्यात्मा चितिशक्तिरेव ज्ञानक्रिया-मायाशक्तिरूपा पशुदशायां संकोचप्रकर्षात् सत्त्व-रजस्तमः-स्वभावचित्तात्मतया स्फुरति; इति श्रीप्रत्यभिज्ञायामुक्तम् । अत एव श्रीतत्त्वगर्भस्तोत्रे विकल्पदशायामपि तात्त्विकस्वरूपसद्भावात् तदनुसरणाभिप्रायेण उक्तम्—

'अत एव तु ये केचित्परमार्थानुसारिणः ।
तेषां तत्र स्वरूपस्य स्वज्योतिष्ट्वं न लुप्यते ॥'

both limitations (i.e. external and internal objects of consciousness) becomes *citta* (individual consciousness). Thus has it been said in the excellent *Pratyabhijñā*.

Jñāna, Kriyā and the third Śakti Māyā of the Lord (Śiva) appear as *sattva, rajas* and *tamas* in the case of *Paśu* (the individual *jiva*) in respect of the objective realities which are like His (Lord's) own limbs.[55] By this and other such statements, (it is clear that) *Citi* (universal consciousness) which is of the nature of absolute freedom and which has the powers of *jñāna, kriyā,* and *māyā* appears owing to excess of limitation in the state of *paśu* (the individual soul) as *Citta* (individual consciousness) which is of the nature of *sattva, rajas,* and *tamas.*[56] This has been stated in *Pratyabhijñā* (i.e. Īśvara-pratyabhijñā of Utpala-deva I. 4, 3).

Because the individual consciousness is, even in the state of Vikalpa,[57] of the nature of the highest real (i.e. Śiva), therefore with a view to pursuing that (*tat* i.e. the Highest Real), it has been said in the excellent *Tattva-garbha-stotra.*

इति ॥ ५ ॥

चित्तमेव तु मायाप्रमातुः स्वरूपम्–इत्याह—

तन्मयो मायाप्रमाता ॥ ६ ॥

देहप्राणपदं तावत् चित्तप्रधानमेव; शून्यभूमिरपि चित्तसंस्कारवत्येव; अन्यथा ततो व्युत्थितस्य स्वकर्तव्यानुधावनाभावः स्यात्;–इति चित्तमय एव मायीयः प्रमाता। अमुनैव आशयेन शिवसूत्रेषु वस्तुवृत्तानुसारेण

'चैतन्यमात्मा' (१—१)

इत्यभिधाय, मायाप्रमातृलक्षणावसरे पुनः

'चित्तमात्मा' (३—१)

"Therefore in all those who are pursuers of the Highest Truth, the self-luminous character of their inmost nature never disappears (in any condition)".

In view of the fact that *citta* alone is the real nature of *Māyāpramātṛ*, it is said—

Sūtra 6. The Māyāpramātṛ[58] consists of it (i.e. Citta).

Commentary

Citta is predominant in the sphere of life and body. The sphere of the void also consists of the *saṁskāras* (impressions, dispositions) of the *Citta*, otherwise one who awakes (from the experience of the void) would not be able to follow one's duties. Therfore, *māyāpramātṛ* consists of *Citta* only. With this purport, in *Śivasūtras*, while discussing reality (*vastu-vṛtta-anusāreṇa*), having said that universal consciousness (*caitanyam*) is the Self, it is again said that "individual consciousness (*cittam*) is the self" when the occasion for discussing the characteristics of *māyāpramātṛ* arises.

इत्युक्तम् ॥ ६ ॥

अस्यैव सम्यक् स्वरूपज्ञानात् यतो मुक्तिः, असम्यक् तु संसारः, ततः तिलश एतत्स्वरूपं निर्भङ्क्तुमाह—

स चैको द्विरूपस्त्रिमयश्चतुरात्मा
सप्तपञ्चकस्वभावः ॥ ७ ॥

निर्णीतदृशा चिदात्मा शिवभट्टारक एव 'एक' आत्मा, न तु अन्यः कश्चित्; प्रकाशस्य देशकालादिभिः भेदायोगात्; जडस्य तु ग्राहकत्वानुपपत्तेः। प्रकाश एव यतः स्वातन्त्र्यात् गृहीतप्राणादिसंकोचः संकुचितार्थग्राहकतामश्नुते, ततः असौ प्रकाशरूपत्वसंकोचावभासवत्त्वाभ्यां 'द्विरूपः'। आणव-मायीय-कार्ममलः-

Since *mukti* or liberation is possible only by a correct knowledge of the true nature of the Self, and transmigration (from life to life) (*saṁsāra*) is due to an incorrect knowledge (thereof), therefore is it proposed to analyse the true nature of it (i.e. the Self) bit by bit—

Sūtra 7. And (though) he is one, he becomes of twofold form, threefold, fourfold, and of the nature of seven pentads.

Commentary

From the point of view of what has already been definitely stated, exalted Śiva only who is of the nature of *Cit* is the one Atmā and none other, because the light (of consciousness) cannot be divided by space and time, and the merely inert cannot be a subject.*

* The meaning is —*jaḍa* or the merely inert can only be an object of experience, not a subject of experience.

वृतत्वात् 'त्रिमयः'। शून्य-प्राण-पुर्यष्टकशरीरस्वभावत्वात् 'चतुरात्मा' सप्त-पञ्चकानि'–शिवादिपृथिव्यन्तानि पञ्चत्रिंशत्तत्त्वानि 'तत्स्वभावः'। तथा शिवादि सकलान्त-प्रमातृसप्तकस्वरूपः; चिदानन्देच्छा-ज्ञान-क्रियाशक्तिरूपत्वेऽपि अख्यातिवशात् कला-विद्या-राग-काल-नियतिकञ्चुकवलितत्वात् पञ्चकस्वरूपः। एवं च शिवैकरूपत्वेन, पञ्चत्रिंशत्तत्त्वमयत्वेन, प्रमातृसप्तकस्वभावत्वेन चिदादि-

Since consciousness (lit., light of consciousness) itself, through the sovereignty of its free will,[59] assumes the limitation of *prāṇa* etc. and the state of the experient of limited objects, therefore is it that it is of twofold form, viz., the manifester i.e. the light of consciousness, and limited manifestation.

Owing to its being covered by the *mala*[60] pertaining to *aṇu*, *māyā*, and *karma*, it becomes threefold.

It (also) becomes fourfold, because of its assuming the nature of (1) *Śūnya*[61] (2) *prāṇa* (3) *puryaṣṭaka*[62] and (4) the gross body.

The seven pentads i.e., the thirty-five *tattvas* (principles), from Śiva down to the earth are (also) its nature (or *sapta* and *pañca* in the sūtra may be taken separately as seven and five). So from *Śiva* down to *sakala*, the consciousness consists of a heptad of experients.§ Though its essential nature is that of *cit* (consciousness), *ānanda* (bliss), *icchā* (will), *jñāna* (knowledge), *kriyā* (action)—a fivefold nature, it becomes of the form of another pentad, limited as it becomes by the coverings of *kalā*, *vidyā*, *rāga*, *kāla*, and *niyati*,[63] owing to *akhyāti* (nescience). Thus only when it is recognized that the one Reality which is only Śiva becomes thirtyfive principles,

§ The seven experients are 1 Śiva-pramātā, 2 Mantra-maheśvara 3 Mantreśvara 4 Mantra, 5 Vijñānākala, 6 Pralayākala, and 7 Sakala.

शक्तिपञ्चकात्मकत्वेन च अयं प्रत्यभिज्ञायमानो मुक्तिदः; अन्यथा तु संसारहेतुः ॥७॥

एवं च

तद्भूमिकाः सर्वदर्शनस्थितयः ॥ ८ ॥

'सर्वेषां' चार्वाकादिदर्शनानां 'स्थितयः'–सिद्धान्ताः 'तस्य' एतस्य आत्मनो नटस्येव स्वेच्छावगृहीताः कृत्रिमा 'भूमिकाः' । तथा च

'चैतन्यविशिष्टं शरीरमात्मा ।'

इति चार्वाकाः

seven experients, a pentad of five powers consisting of *Cit* etc., only then does it become a bestower of (spiritual) liberty; otherwise (i.e. in the absence of this recognition) it is the cause of *saṁsāra* (passing on from existence to existence).

And so

Sūtra 8. The positions of the various systems of philosophy are only various roles of that (Consciousness or Self).

Commentary

The positions i.e. the settled conclusions of all the systems of philosophy, viz., *Cārvākas* and others are, so to speak, this Self's assumed roles accepted of his own accord like the roles accepted by an actor.

Thus the *Cārvākas* (i.e. followers of Cārvāka system) maintain that the Self is identical with the body characterized by consciousness. The followers of Nyāya etc.* consider Self so long as it is in the worldly condition, as practically identical

* By etc. is to be understood *Vaiśeṣika*.

नैयायिकादयो ज्ञानादिगुणगणाश्रयं बुद्धितत्त्वप्रायमेव आत्मानं संसृतौ मन्यन्ते, अपवर्गे तु तदुच्छेदे शून्यप्रायम् ।

अहंप्रतीतिप्रत्येयः सुखदुःखाद्युपाधिभिः तिरस्कृतः आत्मा—इति मन्वाना मीमांसका अपि बुद्धावेव निविष्टाः ।

ज्ञानसंतान एव तत्त्वम्—इति सौगता बुद्धिवृत्तिषु एव पर्यवसिताः ।

प्राण एव आत्मा—इति केचित् श्रुत्यन्तविदः ।

असदेव इदमासीत्—इत्यभावब्रह्मवादिनः शून्यभुवमवगाह्य स्थिताः ।

माध्यमिका अपि एवमेव ।

परा प्रकृतिः भगवान् वासुदेवः तद्विस्फुलिङ्गप्राया एव जीवा –

with *buddhi* (intuitive faculty of certain knowledge) which is the substratum of knowledge, and other qualities. In liberation when *buddhi* disappears, they regard Self as almost identical with the void. The followers of Mīmāṁsā are also tied down to *buddhi* inasmuch as they think that what is known in the cognition of 'I' veiled by the *upādhis*[64] i.e. the limiting conditions of pleasure and pain, is the Self. The followers of Sugata[65] also stop with only the functions of *buddhi*, maintaining that the fundamental principle is only a continuum of cognitions. Some of the followers of Vedānta regard *prāṇa* (the vital principle) as the Self.

The Brahmavādins (advocates of the Veda) who consider non-being (*abhāva*) as the fundamental principle on the ground (of the Upaniṣadic dictum) that 'all this was originally non-being', accept the position of the void, and are (thus) landed in it. The Mādhyamikas[66] are also in the same position.

The Pāñcarātras[67] (believe) that Lord Vāsudeva is the highest cause (*prakṛti*);[68] the individual souls are like sparks

इति पाञ्चरात्राः परस्या प्रकृतेः परिणामाभ्युपगमात् अव्यक्ते एव अभिनिविष्टाः ।

सांख्यादयस्तु विज्ञानाकलप्रायां भूमिमवलम्बन्ते ।

सदेव इदमग्र आसीत्—इति ईश्वरतत्त्वपदमाश्रिता अपरे श्रुत्यन्तविदः ।

शब्दब्रह्ममयं पश्यन्तीरूपम् आत्मतत्त्वम्—इति वैयाकरणाः श्रीसदाशिवपदमध्यासिताः । एवमन्यदपि अनुमन्तव्यम् । एतच्च आगमेषु

'बुद्धितत्त्वे स्थिता बौद्धा गुणेष्वेवार्हताः स्थिताः ।
स्थिता वेदविदः पुंसि अव्यक्ते पाञ्चरात्रिकाः ॥'

इत्यादिना निरूपितम् ।

of him, and so assuming the individual souls as transformation[69] of the highest cause, they cling to the non-manifest[70] (as the source of every thing).

The Sāṅkhyas[71] and others (of similar views) cling to the stage characterized mostly by the Vijñānākalas.[72]

Other knowers of Vedānta cling to Īśvara-principle (as the highest) status, (depending as they do on the Upaniṣadic dictum)—"Being alone was there in the beginning."

The exponents of Vyākaraṇa,[73] considering Ātman (Self) principle as *śabda-brahman*[74] in the form of *paśyantī*[75] attribute the highest reality to the status of Śrī Sadāśiva. Likewise other systems may also be inferred (to represent only a part of our system). This has also been described in the Āgamas[76] (in the following verse) :

"The Buddhists rest content with the Buddhi principle, the Ārhatas[77] with the *guṇas*, the Veda-knowers with the Puruṣa and the Pāñcarātrikas with *avyakta*."

विश्वोत्तीर्णमात्मतत्त्वम्–इति तान्त्रिकाः ।
विश्वमयम् इति–कुलाद्याम्नायनिविष्टाः ।
विश्वोत्तीर्णं विश्वमयं च—इति त्रिकादि दर्शनविदः ।

एवम् एकस्यैव चिदात्मनो भगवतः स्वातन्त्र्यावभासिताः सर्वा इमा भूमिकाः स्वातन्त्र्यप्रच्छादनोन्मीलनतारतम्यभेदिताः । अत एक एव एतावद्व्याप्तिक आत्मा । मितदृष्टयस्तु अंशांशिकासु तदिच्छयैव अभिमानं ग्राहिताः येन देहादिषु भूमिषु पूर्वपूर्वप्रमातृव्याप्तिसारताप्रथायामपि उक्तरूपां महाव्याप्तिं परशक्तिपातं विना न लभन्ते । यथोक्तम्—

The Tāntrikas[79] manitain that the *ātman* principle transcends the universe. Those who are wedded to the sacred texts of Kula[80] etc. consider that the *ātman* principle is steeped in the universe (i.e. that the universe is only a form of the Ātman). The knowers of Trika[81] philosophy etc., however, maintain that the *ātman* principle is both immanent in the universe and transcends it.

Thus of the one Divine whose essence is consciousness, all these roles are displayed by his absolute will, (and) the differences in the roles are due to the various gradations in which that absolute free will either chooses to reveal or conceal itself. Therefore there is one Ātman only pervading all these (roles).

Those of limited vision, however, in various parts are caused to identify themselves with the various (limited) stages by His will on account of which, even though when it is made clear that the the essential reason of the erroneous concepts of the preceding experients lies in their identification with the body etc., they are unable to comprehend the great pervasion (of the Ātman) described above (by *Trika* philosophy, viz., that the *Ātman* is both immanent in the universe and transcends it) unless the Śakti[82] of the Highest descend upon them (i.e. without the grace of the Highest). As has been said—

'वैष्णवाद्यास्तु ये केचिद्विद्यारागेण रञ्जिताः ।
न विदन्ति परं देवं सर्वज्ञं ज्ञानशालिनम् ॥'

इति । तथा

'भ्रमयत्येव तान्माया ह्यमोक्षे मोक्षलिप्सया ।'

इति ।

'त आत्मोपासकाः शैवं न गच्छन्ति परं पदम् ॥'

इति च ।

अपि च 'सर्वेषां दर्शनानां'–समस्तानां नीलसुखाविज्ञानानां याः 'स्थितयः' –अन्तर्मुखरूपा विश्रान्तयः ताः 'तद्भूमिकाः' –चिदानन्दघनस्वात्मस्वरूपाभिव्यक्त्युपायाः । तथा हि यदा यदा बहिर्मुखं रूपं स्वरूपे विश्राम्यति, तदा तदा बाह्य-

"The Vaiṣṇavas and others who are coloured (i.e. whose minds are coloured) by the attachment or colour of *Vidyā*,[83] do not know the highest God, the omniscient, full of knowledge. Likewise, (it has been said) in *Svacchanda Tantra*, (10th Paṭala, verse 1141)—

It is only *Māyā* which whirls these (followers of other systems) round who desire to obtain liberation (*mokṣa*) in non-liberation (i.e. in those disciplines and scriptures which are incapable of offering liberation)" and also, (it has been said in *Netra Tantra*, 8th Paṭala, verse 30) "Those who are attached to the limited as the Self (e.g., the body as Self, the *buddhi* as Self etc.) do not reach the highest stage of Śiva".* Also (There is another interpretation of the *sūtra* : *Darśana* is to be interpreted, not as a system of philosophy, but merely as knowledge; *sthiti*, not as stage, but as inward cessation; *bhūmikā* — not as role, but as means — the whole interpretation is as follows) :The

---

*Prof. Leidecker's translation — "The worshippers of *ātman* do not reach the highest place" is to say the least, highly misleading. It is not the worshippers of the Self who do not reach the highest stage, but those who consider the body, buddhi etc. as Self.

वस्तूपसंहारः; अन्तः प्रशान्तपदावस्थितिः; तत्तदुदेष्यत्संवित्संतत्यासूत्रणम्; – इति सृष्टि-स्थिति-संहारमेलनरूपा इयं तुरीया संविद्भट्टारिका तत्तत्सृष्ट्यादिभेदान् उद्वमन्ती संहरन्ती च, सदा पूर्णा च, कृशा च, उभयरूपा च अनुभयात्मा च, अक्रममेव स्फुरन्ती स्थिता । उक्तं च श्रीप्रत्यभिज्ञाटीकायाम्—

'तावदर्थविलेहेन उत्तष्ठिति, पूर्णा च भवति'

sthitis i.e. the inward *cessation* of all darśanas i.e. all empirical knowledge, e.g., the experience of (an external thing as) colour, like blue, or an (inner) experience like, pleasure etc. becomes a means of the manifestation of the essential nature of *tat* i.e., Śiva who is of the nature of consciousness and mass of bliss. So, whenever the external form (of consciousness) comes to rest in the essential nature (of the knower), there ensues the cessation of the external thing (*saṁhāra*), resting in a condition of inner peace, and then commencement of a continuous series of various experiences (*saṁvit-santati*) which will be arising anew (*udeṣyat*). Thus this venerable *turīyā*[84] (fourth) consciousness whose nature it is to hold together emanation, maintenance and re-absorption flashes forth ceaselessly (lit. without succession) now sending forth diversities of various emanations (created things), and now withdrawing (them) — always emaciated and yet always full, of both forms (i.e. both emaciated and full) and also not undergoing any of these forms.* It has been said in *Śrī Pratyabhijñā-ṭīkā* — "When re-absorbing the objects, she (Śakti) flashes (lit. rises) (in Her

*This exhausts all the four alternatives. The idea is that though *turīyā Saṁvid* goes on projecting things out of herself (which shows that she is perfectly full and rich), and re-absorbing them into herself (which shows that she is depleted and must take back things in order to make up her loss), yet in herself she transcends all these alternatives.

इति । एषा च भट्टारिका क्रमात्क्रमम् अधिकमनुशील्यमाना स्वात्मसात्करोत्येव भक्तजनम् ॥८॥

यदि एवंभूतस्य आत्मनो विभूतिः, तत् कथम् अयं मलावृतः अणुः कलाविवलितः संसारी अभिधीयते ?—इत्याह—

चिद्वत्तच्छक्तिसंकोचात् मलावृतः संसारी ॥ ९ ॥

यदा 'चिदात्मा' परमेश्वरः स्वस्वातन्त्र्यात् अभेदव्याप्तिं निमज्य भेदव्याप्तिम् अवलम्बते, तदा 'तदीया इच्छादिशक्तयः' असंकुचिता अपि 'संकोचवत्यो' भान्ति; तदानीमेव च अयं 'मलावृतः संसारी' भवति । तथा च अप्रति-

nature), and so she is full."† This venerable (power) being resorted to more and more makes her devotee her own step by step.

If *ātman* (Self) who is as described (above), who has (such) greatness, how is it said to be an *aṇu* (jīva) covered with *mala*,[85] enclosed with *kalā*[86] and other *kañcukas*, a *saṁsārin* (transmigrating from one life to another). (In answer to this question), it is said (lit. he, the author says):

Sūtra 9. In consequence of its limitation of Śakti,§ reality which is all consciousness, becomes the mala-covered samsārin.

Commentary

When the highest Lord whose very essence is consciousness, conceals by His free will, pervasion of non-duality, and assumes duality all round, then His will and other powers,

† Prof. Leidecker says that *avaleha* (i.e. licking) is meaningless here and suggests the reading *avahela*. But the reading *avaleha* is perfectly correct. It means licking, devouring i.e. re-absorbing the objects. Space, time and objects are devoured by *Turīyā* in which only I-consciousness remains.

§ Prof. Leidecker translates *cid-vat* as cit-like. The *vat* suffix does not connote likeness here, but means 'full of' *cidvat* means the ultimate Principle which is all consciousness. Śiva is not *cit*-like but all *cit*. Kṣemarāja also explains *cidvat* as "*cidātma*" in his commentary on this Sūtra.

हृतस्वातन्त्र्यरूपा इच्छाशक्तिः संकुचिता सती अपूर्णमन्यतारूपम् आणवं मलम्; ज्ञानशक्तिः क्रमेण संकोचात् भेदे सर्वज्ञत्वस्य किंचिज्ज्ञत्वाप्तेः अन्तःकरण-बुद्धीन्द्रियतापत्तिपूर्वम् अत्यन्तं संकोचग्रहणेन भिन्नवेद्यप्रथारूपं मायीयं मलम्; क्रियाशक्तिः क्रमेण भेदे सर्वकर्तृत्वस्य किंचित्कर्तृत्वाप्तेः कर्मेन्द्रियरूप-संकोचग्रहणपूर्वम् अत्यन्तं परिमिततां प्राप्ता शुभाशुभानुष्ठानमयं कार्मं मलम्। तथा सर्वकर्तृत्व-सर्वज्ञत्व-पूर्णत्व-नित्यत्व-व्यापकत्वशक्तयः संकोचं गृह्णाना यथाक्रमं कला-विद्या-राग-काल-

though essentially non-limited assume limitation. Then only does this (soul) become a transmigratory being, covered with *mala*. Thus the Will-power (of the Absolute) whose sovereignty is unrestricted, assuming limitation, becomes *āṇava-mala*, which consists in its considering itself imperfect. (In the case of) knowledge-power, owing to its becoming gradually limited in the world of differentiation, its omniscience becomes reduced to knowledge of a few things (only). By assuming extreme limitation beginning with the acquisition of an inner organ, and organs of perception, it acquires *māyīya-mala*[87] which consists in the apprehension of all objects as different. (In the case of) action-power, its omnipotence, in this world of differentiation, becomes reduced to the doership of a few things (only), and starting with assuming limitation in the form of organs of action, it becomes extremely limited, and acquires *kārma-mala*[88] which consists in doing good or evil. Thus by accepting limitation, the *śaktis* (powers) omnipotence, omniscience, perfection, eternity, omnipresence appear respectively as *kalā* (limited agency), *vidyā* (limitation in respect of knowledge), *rāga* (limitation in respect of desire) *kāla* (limitation in respect of time), and *niyati* (limitation in respect of space and cause).[89] Thus constituted this (*ātman* or Self) is called *saṁsārin* (a transmigratory being), poor

नियतिरूपतया भान्ति। तथाविधश्च अयं शक्तिदरिद्रः संसारी उच्यते; स्वशक्तिविकासे तु शिव एव ॥६॥

नन्‌ संसार्यवस्थायाम्‌ अस्य किंचित्‌ शिवतोचितम्‌ अभिज्ञानमस्ति येन शिव एव तथावस्थितः ?—इत्युद्‌घोष्यते । अस्ति इत्याह—

तथापि तद्वत्‌ पञ्च कृत्यानि करोति ॥१०॥

इह ईश्वराद्वयदर्शनस्य ब्रह्मवादिभ्यः अयमेव विशेषः, यत्‌

'सृष्टिसंहारकर्तारं विलयस्थितिकारकम्‌ ।

in Śakti. With the (full) unfoldment of his *śaktis*, however, he is Śiva himself.

Well, is there any mark appropriate to Śiva-state by which the Self even in the *saṁsārin*-stage may be recognised as Śiva himself appearing in that condition ? It is declared, "There is", (and so the next *sūtra*) says :

Sūtra 10. "Even in this condition (of the empirical self), he (the individual) does the five kṛtyas (deeds) like Him (i.e. like Siva)."

Commentary

Here, the distinction between the *Īśvarādvaya*[90] philosophy from (that of) the Brahmavādins[91] lies in this—that the divine whose essence is consciousness* always retains his authorship of the fivefold act which[92] is in accordance with what has been stated by the grand *Svacchanda* and other disciplines (of Śaiva philosophy), viz., (Vide. *Svacchanda Tantra* 1st Paṭala, 3rd verse) "(I bow to the) Divine who brings about (1) emanation (*sṛṣṭi*), (2) re-absorption (*saṁhāra*), (3) concealment

* Cidātman does not mean *cit*-like as Prof. Leidecker has translated it, but 'whose essence is *cit* or consciousness'.

अनुग्रहकरं देवं प्रणतार्तिविनाशनम् ॥'

इति श्रीमत्स्वच्छन्दादिशासनोक्तनीत्या सदा पञ्चविधकृत्यकारित्वं चिदात्मनो भगवतः। यथा च भगवान् शुद्धेतराध्वस्फारणक्रमेण स्वरूपविकासरूपाणि सृष्ट्यादीनि करोति, 'तथा' संकुचितचिच्छक्तितया संसारभूमिकायामपि 'पञ्चकृत्यानि' विधत्ते। तथा हि

'तदेवं व्यवहारेऽपि प्रभुर्देहादिमाविशन्।
भान्तमेवान्तरर्थौघमिच्छया भासयेद्बहिः ॥'

इति प्रत्यभिज्ञाकारिकोक्तार्थदृष्ट्या देहप्राणादिपदम् आविशन् चिद्रूपो महेश्वरो बहिर्मुखीभावावसरे नीलादिकमर्थं नियतदेशकालादितया यदा

(*vilaya*), (4) maintenance (of the world) (*sthiti*), who dispenses, (5) grace (*anugraha*), and who destroys the affliction of those who have bowed down (to Him)".*

Just as the Exalted One (Śiva) by the process of expansion in the extrinsic course[93] (i.e. mundane manifestation) brings about emanation etc., which are an unfoldment of his real nature, so does He carry out the five processes even in the condition of *saṁsāra*, by limiting His consciousness-power. So that (as it has been said) (in *Īśvarapratyabhijñā*, VI Āhnika, 7th verse).

"This being the position (*tat evam*, here means, *tat evam sati*), even in the empirical state (*vyavahare'pi*), the Lord entering into the body etc., causes the objects (lit. collection of objects) to appear outwardly by His Will though appearing within Himself." (The fivefold processes in the condition of the world are shown below).

Thus according to the view-point of *Pratyabhijñākārikā*, when the great Lord who is consciousness (lit. whose form is consciousness) entering into the sphere of the body, *prāṇa*

---

* Curiously enough, Prof. Leidecker has translated *praṇatārti-vināśanam* as 'him whom destruction of sorrow is subordinated' which hardly makes any sense.

आभासयति, तदा नियतदेशकालाद्याभासांशे अस्य स्रष्टृता; अन्यदेशकालाद्याभासांशे अस्य संहर्तृता; नीलाद्याभासांशे स्थापकता; भेदेन आभासांशे विलयकारिता; प्रकाशैक्येन प्रकाशने अनुग्रहीतृता। यथा च सदा पञ्चविधकृत्यकारित्वं भगवतः, तथा मया वितत्य स्पन्दसंदोहे निर्णीतम्।

एवमिदं पञ्चविधकृत्यकारित्वम् आत्मीयं सदा दृढप्रतिपत्त्या परिशील्यमानं माहेश्वर्यम् उन्मीलयत्येव भक्तिभाजाम्। अत एव ये सदा एतत् परिशीलयन्ति, ते स्वरूपविकासमयं विश्वं जानाना जीवन्मुक्ता इत्याम्नाताः। ये तु न

etc. on the occasion of the attention becoming external, makes objects like blue etc. appear in definite space, time etc. then with reference to appearance in definite space, time etc., it is His act of emanation (*sraṣṭṛtā*). With reference to the appearance of the objects in another space, time etc., it is His act of withdrawal or absorption (*saṁhartṛtā*). With reference to the actual (continuity of the) appearance of blue etc., it is His act of maintenance (*sthāpakatā*). With reference to its appearance as different, it is His act of concealment[94] (*vilayakāritā*). With reference to the appearance of every thing as identical with the light (of consciousness),[95] it is His act of grace (*anugrahītṛtā*). As to how the Lord is always the author of the fivefold act, I have extensively demonstrated in *Spandasandoha*. Thus this authorship of the fivefold act occurring within one's own personal experience, if pursued steadily with firm understanding, reveals the Lord's greatness to the devotee. Therefore, those who always ponder over this (fivefold act of the Lord), knowing the universe as an unfoldment of the essential nature (of consciousness), become liberated in this very life. This is what the (sacred) tradition maintains (*ityāmnātāḥ*). Those who do not ponder like this,

तथा, ते सर्वतो विभिन्नं मेयजातं पश्यन्तो बद्धात्मानः ॥१०॥

न च अयमेव प्रकारः पञ्चविधकृत्यकारित्वे, यावत् अन्योऽपि कश्चित् रहस्यरूपोऽस्ति । इत्याह—

आभासन-रक्ति-विमर्शन-बीजावस्थापन-
विलापनतस्तानि ॥ ११ ॥

'पञ्चविधकृत्यानि करोति' इति पूर्वतः संबध्यते । श्रीमन्महार्थदृष्ट्या दृगादिदेवीप्रसरणक्रमेण यत् यत् आभाति, तत् तत् सृज्यते; तथा सृष्टे पदे तत्र

seeing all objects of experience as essentially different, remain for ever bound.*

This is not the only mode of the authorship of the fivefold act, there exists another esoteric mode, besides this. So, he says (i.e. it is said):

Sūtra 11. As Manifesting, relishing, experiencing as self, settling of the seed, dissolution, these.

Commentary

These i.e. these fivefold acts,[96] he does — this is (syntactically) connected with the previous. From the point of view of the highest end (*mahārthadṛṣṭyā*),[97] whatever appears through the successive functioning (lit. expansion) of the goddess of sight and other (perceptual functions) is, (so to speak) emanated (*sṛjyate*) (this is *ābhāsana* or manifesting). An

*Prof. Leidecker gives a very curious translation of this — "Those, however, who do not likewise behold the totality of objects differentiated everywhere" — This is just the opposite of what is meant. In fact, a comma is implied after *tathā*. This is the reading adopted by the Kashmir Sanskrit Series.

यदा प्रशान्तनिमेषं कंचित् कालं रज्यति, तदा स्थितिदेव्या तत् स्थाप्यते; चमत्कारापरपर्यायविमर्शनसमये संह्रियते । यथोक्तं श्रीरामेण

'समाधिवज्रेणाप्यन्यैरभेद्यो भेदभूधरः ।
परामृष्टश्च नष्टश्च त्वद्भक्तिबलशालिभिः ।।

इति । यदा तु संह्रियमाणमपि एतत् अन्तः विचित्राशङ्कादिसंस्कारम् आधत्ते, तदा तत् पुनः उद्भविष्यत्संसारबीजभावमापन्नं विलयपदम् अध्यारोपितम् । यदा पुनः तत् तथा अन्तः स्थापितम् अन्यत् वा अनुभूयमानमेव हठपाक-

object being thus emanated (i.e. brought forth into appearance), when (the Self) without shutting of the eye relishes it for some time, it is maintained (in experience) till then by the goddess of maintenance. (This relishing of the experience for sometime represents *sthiti* or maintenance). It is withdrawn at the time of *vimarśa* (*vimarśana-samaye*) for which another word is sudden flash of delight (*camatkāra*).[98] (This knowledge of the object represents *saṁhāra*).[99] As it has been said by Rāma

"The mountain of manifoldness which cannot be split by others even by the thunderbolt of contemplation (*Samādhi*, lit. collectedness of consciousness) is experienced as oneself and thus destroyed by those who are endowed with the power that accrues from devotion to you".

However, if at the time of the re-absorption or withdrawal (of the experience of manifoldness or differentiation), it (i.e. the object of experience) generates various *saṁskāras* (impressions) of doubt etc. inwardly, then it acquires the state of *saṁsāra* in germ which is bound to spring forth into existence again, and thus it super-poses (on the experient) the state of *vilaya* (concealment of the real nature of the Self). On the other hand while it (i.e. the world which has been reduced to a germinal form) is being held inwardly and anything else that is experienced at that time, if it is burned to sameness with the fire of consciousness, by the process of

क्रमेण अलंग्रासयुक्त्या चिदग्निसाद्भावम् आपद्यते, तदा पूर्णतापादनेन अनुगृह्णाते एव। ईदृशं च पञ्चविधकृत्यकारित्वं सर्वस्य सदा संनिहितमपि सद्गुरूपदेशं विना न प्रकाशते, इति सद्गुरुसपर्यैव एतत्प्रथार्थम् अनुसर्तव्या ॥११॥

यस्य पुनः सद्गुरूपदेशं विना एतत्परिज्ञानं नास्ति, तस्य अवच्छादितस्वस्वरूपाभिः निजाभिः शक्तिभिः व्यामोहितत्वं भवति। इत्याह

तदपरिज्ञाने स्वशक्तिभिर्व्यामोहितता
संसारित्वम् ॥ १२ ॥

'तस्य' एतस्य सदा संभवतः पञ्चविधकृत्यकारित्वस्य 'अपरिज्ञाने'–

haṭhapāka[100] and by the device of *alaṁgrāsa*,[101] then by bringing about perfection, he (the yogin) enters the state of grace. This kind of the authorship of the fivefold act, though always near at hand to every body, does not become manifest without the instruction of a good *guru* (i.e. a spiritual master). One should, therefore, take to the reverential service of a good *guru* in order that this (i.e. the experience of the fivefold act) may become manifest to him.

He, however, who does not acquire the complete knowledge (of the authorship of the fivefold act) owing to the lack of guidance from a good *guru* remains deluded by his own powers (*śaktis*) since the real nature of every one (of these *śaktis*) is concealed (from him). Therefore it is said :

Sūtra 12. To be a saṁsārin means being deluded by one's own powers because of the ignorance of that (authorship of the fivefold act).

Commentary

'*Tat*' i.e. of that (in the *sūtra*) means the authorship of this fivefold act which is always happening; '*aparijñāne*' or

शक्तिपातहेतुकस्वबलोन्मीलनाभावात् अप्रकाशने 'स्वाभिः शक्तिभिः व्यामोहितत्वं'-विविधलौकिकशास्त्रीयशङ्काशङ्कुकीलितत्वं यत्, इदमेव 'संसारित्वम्' । तदुक्तं श्रीसर्ववीरभट्टारके

'अज्ञानाच्छङ्कते लोकस्ततः सृष्टिश्च संहृतिः ॥

इति ।

'मन्त्रा वर्णात्मकाः सर्वे सर्वे वर्णाः शिवात्मकाः ॥

इति च । तथा हि—चित्प्रकाशात् अव्यतिरिक्ता नित्योदितमहामन्त्ररूपा पूर्णाहंविमर्शमयी या इयं परा वाक्शक्तिः आदि-क्षान्त-रूपाशेषशक्तिचक्रगर्भिणी. सा तावत् पश्यन्तीमध्यमाविक्रमेण ग्राहकभूमिकां भासयति । तत्र च परारूपत्वेन

ignorance means 'not flashing forth' on account of the absence of the manifestation of one's own power which becomes effective through the descent of *Śakti*. (The rest of the *sūtra* means)—acquiring the condition of a *saṁsārin* (transmigrant) which is due to delusion (*vyāmohitatvam*) (which means) being nailed by various doubts created by the *śāstras* (scriptural text), and worldly opinions.

It has been said in the excellent *Sarvavīrabhaṭṭāraka*:

"Through ignorance people are subject to uncertainty; hence follow birth and death". Again,

"The essence of all *mantras*[102] consists in letters or sounds, (and) the essence of all letters or sounds is Śiva".

Now then the *vākśakti* (power of speech) (known as) *parā*[103] (supreme) who is identical with the light of consciousness (i.e. Śiva), who is of the form of great *mantra* that is eternally sounded, who consists of the consciousness of the perfect 'I', who contains within herself (lit. who is pregnant with) the whole assemblage of *śaktis* formed by the sounds beginning with '*a*' and ending with '*kṣa*',[104] brings into manifestation the sphere

स्वरूपम् अप्रथयन्ती मायाप्रमातुः अस्फुटासाधारणार्थाविभासरूपां प्रतिक्षण नवनवां विकल्पक्रियामुल्लासयति, शुद्धामपि च अविकल्पभूमिं तदाच्छादितामेव दर्शयति। तत्र च ब्राह्म्यादिदेवताधिष्ठितककारादिविचित्रशक्तिभिः व्यामोहितो देहप्राणादिमेव परिमितम् अवशम् आत्मानं मन्यते मूढजनः। ब्राह्म्यादिदेव्यः पशुदशायां भेदविषये सृष्टिस्थिती, अभेदविषये च संहारं प्रथयन्त्यः, परिमितविकल्पपात्रतामेव संपादयन्ति; पतिदशायां तु भेदे संहारम् अभेदे च सर्गस्थिती प्रकटयन्त्यः, क्रमात्क्रमं विकल्पनिर्ह्रासनेन श्रीमद्भैरवमुद्रानुप्रवेशमयीं महतीम् अविकल्पभूमिमेव उन्मीलयन्ति।

of the (limited) subject or experient through the successive phases of *paśyanti*,[105] *madhyamā* etc. In this state (of the limited experient) she conceals her real form as *parā* and produces in the empirical subject (*māyā-pramātuḥ*) ever-new *vikalpa*-activity[106] every moment which activity brings into view objects that are obscure and particular, and also she presents the stage of *avikalpa*[107] as veiled by that (*vikalpa*-activity), though in itself it (the *avikalpa* stage) is quite pure. In these circumstances, and deluded by the peculiar *Śaktis* in the form of '*ka*' and other consonants which are presided over by Brāhmī[108] and other deities, the deluded man helplessly considers the body, *prāṇas* etc. themselves which are limited as the Self.

Brāhmī and the other deities, in the stage of *paśu* (the bound soul), manifesting emanation and maintenance in respect of differences, and withdrawal in respect of non-difference, bring about only fitness for limited *vikalpas*. In the *pati* (lord) stage, however, these (deities) manifesting withdrawal in respect of difference and emanation and maintenance in respect of non-difference,[109] gradually by reducing the *vikalpas*, (ultimately) disclose the great *avikalpa* stage which enables one to enter into the blissful *bhairava-mudrā*,[110] at which stage, they (the *śaktis*) cause to appear the *pure vikalpa śakti*[111] which is deeply merged in consciousness and bliss (which enables one to feel like the following) ·

'सर्वो ममायं विभव इत्येवं परिजानतः ।
विश्वात्मनो विकल्पानां प्रसरेऽपि महेशता ।।'

इत्यादिरूपां चिदानन्दावेशमग्नां शुद्धविकल्पशक्तिम् उल्लासयन्ति ततः उक्तनीत्या स्वशक्तिव्यामोहिततैव संसारित्वम् ।

किंच चितिशक्तिरेव भगवती विश्ववमनात् संसारवामाचारत्वाच्च वामेश्वर्याख्या सती, खेचरी-गोचरी-दिक्चरी-भूचरीरूपैः अशेषैः प्रमातृ-अन्तःकरणबहिष्करण-भावस्वभावैः परिस्फुरन्ती, पशुभूमिकायां शून्यपदविश्रान्ता किंचित्कर्तृत्वाद्यात्मक-कलादिशक्त्यात्मना खेचरीचक्रेण गोपितपारमार्थिक-चिद्गगनचरीत्वस्वरूपेण चकास्ति; भेदनिश्चयाभिमान-विकल्पनप्रधानान्तः-

"He who knows that all this glory (of manifestation) is mine (i. e. belongs to the spirit), who realizes that the entire cosmos is his Self, possesses *maheśatā*[112] even when the *vikalpas*[113] have their play." (*Īśvara-pratyabhijñā*, Āgamādhikāra II Āhnika, 12th verse). Hence the state of a *saṁsārin* (transmigrant) consists, as explained above, in the delusion brought about by one's own *śaktis*.

[The above is known as *Śāmbhavopāya* or the *Śāmbhava*-technique of attaining unity-consciousness. Below is given the *Śāktopāya* or the *Śākta*-technique.]

Further, the exalted consciousness-power (*citi-sakti*) known as Vāmeśvarī,[114] because she emits (i.e. projects) the universe and also because she has to do with the contrary course of *saṁsāra*, displays herself wholly in the condition of the bound subject (*paśu*), as the (empirical) subject in the form of *khecari*,[115] as inner organ in the form of *gocari*, as outer organ in the form of *dikcari*, and as objective existents in the form of *bhūcari*. Resting in the stage of the void (i.e. concealing the true nature of the Self), she shines forth, having concealed her highest reality as *cid-gagana-cari* through the *khecarī* group which consists in the śakti of *kalā* etc., i. e. of the nature of

करणदेवीरूपेण गोचरीचक्रेण गोपिताभेदनिश्चयाद्यात्मकपारमार्थिकस्वरूपेण प्रकाशते; भेदालोचनादिप्रधानबहिष्करणदेवतात्मना च दिक्चरीचक्रेण गोपिताभेदप्रथात्मकपारमार्थिकस्वरूपेण स्फुरति; सर्वतो व्यवच्छिन्नाभासस्वभावप्रमेयात्मना च भूचरीचक्रेण गोपितसार्वात्म्यस्वरूपेण पशुहृदयव्यामोहिना भाति । पतिभूमिकायां तु सर्वकर्तृत्वादिशक्त्यात्मकचिद्गगनचरीत्वेन, अभेदनिश्चयाद्यात्मना गोचरीत्वेन, अभेदालोचनाद्यात्मना दिक्चरीत्वेन, स्वाङ्गकल्पाद्वयप्रथासारप्रमेयात्मना च भूचरीत्वेन पतिहृदयविकासिना स्फुरति । तथा च उक्तं सहजचमत्कारपरिजनिताकृतकादरेण भट्टदामोदरेण विमुक्तकेषु-

'पूर्णाविच्छिन्नमात्रान्तर्बहिष्करणभावगाः ।

limited doership etc. She appears through the *gocarī* group in the form of the deity *antaḥ-karaṇa*[116] (the inner psychic apparatus) whose main functions are ascertainment of difference (*bheda-niścaya*), (in its aspect of *buddhi*) identification (of the Self) with different things (*bheda-abhimāna*), and ideation of things as different (*bheda-vikalpana*), (in its aspect of *manas*) by concealing her real nature which consists in the ascertainment of non-difference etc. She also appears through the *dikcarī* group, in the form of the deity of the outer senses whose main function is perception of difference and so forth, by concealing her real nature which consists in the manifestation of non-difference. She appears, through the *bhūcarī* group in the form of knowable objects which have the nature of differentiated appearances all round, by concealing the real nature of Universal Self, and deluding the heart of creatures.*

In the *pati* stage, however, the *śakti* manifests herself as

---

* Though *cakra* means group, assemblage, or wheel, it suggests an array of forces (like an array of army) in the individual which has to be pierced through before he can ascend to universal consciousness. It is difficult to bring out this subtle suggestion in the translation.

वामेशाद्याः परिज्ञानाज्ञानात्स्युर्मुक्तिबन्धदाः ॥'

इति एवं च निजशक्तिव्यामोहिततैव संसारित्वम् ।

अपि च चिदात्मनः परमेश्वरस्य स्वा अनपायिनी एकैव स्फुरत्तासार-कर्तृतात्मा ऐश्वर्यशक्तिः । सा यदा स्वरूपं गोपयित्वा पाशवे पदे प्राणापान-समान-शक्तिदशाभिः जाग्रत्स्वप्न-सुषुप्तभूमिभिः देहप्राण-पुर्यष्टककलाभिश्च व्यामोहयति, तदा तद्व्यामोहितता संसारित्वम्; यदा तु मध्यधामोल्लासाम्

cidgaganacarī whose essence consists in universal doership, as *gocarī* whose essence consists in the *ascertainment* of non-difference etc., as *dikcarī* whose essence consists in the *perception* of non-difference etc., as *bhūcarī* whose essence consists in (revealing) objects as non-different like limbs of one-self — all these opening up the heart of *pati*.

Venerable Dāmodara, who commands unfeigned respect due to (lit. born of) his innate *camatkāra* (bliss), says in the Vimuktakas i.e., (independent verses) likewise. "Vāmeśa (Vāmeśvarī) and other goddesses having their sphere in the knowing subject (as khecarī), in his inner organ (as gocarī), in the outer senses (as dikcarī) and in objective existences (as bhūcarī), bring about liberation by full knowledge (*parijñāna*), thus making him whole (*pūrṇa*) and bondage by ignorance (*ajñāna*), thus making him limited (*avacchinna*). So, being a *saṁsārin* consists in being deluded by one's own *śaktis.*

[Below is given the *āṇavopāya* — the āṇava-technique of attaining unity-consciousness.]

Again the highest Lord whose essential nature is consciousness has his own *aiśvarya-śakti*[117] which is unique, unfailing and whose essential nature consists in doership[118] which is essentially a *sphurattā* or flashing forth[119] of divine light. When she (i.e. *aiśvaryaśakti*) by concealing her real nature causes delusion in the *paśu* state (i.e. the state of a limited, bound

उदानशक्ति, विश्वव्याप्तिसारां च व्यानशक्ति, तुर्यदशारूपां तुर्यातीतदशारूपां च चिदानन्दघनाम् उन्मीलयति तदा देहाद्यवस्थायामपि पतिदशात्मा जीवन्मुक्तिर्भवति । एवं त्रिधा स्वशक्तिव्यामोहितता व्याख्याता । 'चिद्वत्' इति (९) सूत्रे चित्प्रकाशो गृहीतसंकोचः संसारी इत्युक्तम्, इह तु स्वशक्तिव्यामोहितत्वेन अस्य संसारित्वं भवति,—इति भङ्ग्यन्तरेण उक्तम् । एवं संकुचितशक्तिः प्राणादिमानपि यदा स्वशक्तिव्यामोहितो न भवति तदा अयम्

'............शरीरी परमेश्वरः ।'

इत्याम्नायस्थित्या शिवभट्टारक एव,—इति भङ्ग्या निरूपितं भवति । यदागमः

individual) by the phases of *prāṇa*, *apāna*, and *samāna śaktis*,[120] by the states of waking, dream and deep sleep, and by the *kalās*[121] of the body, *prāṇa* and *puryaṣṭaka*,[122] then this delusion caused by her is the condition of one's being a *saṁsārin* (transmigrating from life to life). When, however, she unfolds the *udāna-śakti*[123] that appears in *madhyadhāma*[124] as of the nature of *turya*[125] state and *vyānaśakti*[126] whose essence is to pervade the universe and which appears as of the nature of *turyātīta*,[127] and both of which are a mass of consciousness and bliss, then even in the state of body etc. one reaches the stage of *pati*[128] and attains liberation while still living.

Thus 'being deluded by one's own *śaktis* (powers)' has been interpreted in three ways.

In the *cidvat sūtra*[129] (*sūtra* 9), it has been said that the light of consciousness itself assuming limitation becomes a *saṁsārin* (an individual migrating from one conditioned existence to another). Here it has been said from a different angle that

'मनुष्यदेहमास्थाय छन्नास्ते परमेश्वराः ।

इति । उक्तं च प्रत्यभिज्ञाटीकायाम्

'शरीरमेव घटाद्यपि वा ये षट्त्रिंशत्तत्त्वमयं शिवरूपतया पश्यन्ति
तेऽपि सिध्यन्ति'

इति ॥ १२ ॥

उक्तसूत्रार्थप्रातिपक्ष्येण तत्त्वदृष्टिं दर्शयितुमाह

तत्परिज्ञाने चित्तमेव अन्तर्मुखीभावेन
चेतनपदाध्यारोहात् चितिः ॥१३॥

it becomes a *saṁsārin* owing to its being deluded by its own powers. It may be observed from another angle that one with limited powers (i.e. an individual soul) in spite of his having *prāṇa* and other (limitations), when not deluded by one's own powers, becomes, according to the thesis of the sacred tradition the Lord (Himself) with a body, or in other words, he can be described as the venerable Śiva Himself. As the Āgama says :

"They are the highest Lord in a veiled from, having entered a human body."

It has also been said in a commentary[130] on the *Pratyabhijñā*.

"They also attain to perfection who consider the body or even the jar etc. consisting of the thirty-six *tattvas* (principles) as a form of Śiva."

In order to show the essential truth, the meaning of the above *sūtra* has been put conversely (in the following) :

Sūtra 13. Acquiring the full knowledge of it (i.e. of the authorship of the five-fold act of the Self), citta[131] itself (i.e. the individual consciousness) by inward movement becomes citi[132] (i.e. universal consciousness) by rising to the status of cetana,[133]

पूर्वसूत्रव्याख्याप्रसङ्गेन प्रमेयदृष्ट्या वितत्य व्याख्यातप्रायमेतत् सूत्रम्; शब्दसंगत्या तु अधुना व्याख्यायते। 'तस्य' आत्मीयस्य पञ्चकृत्यकारित्वस्य 'परिज्ञाने' सति अपरिज्ञानलक्षणकारणापगमात् स्वशक्तिव्यामोहिततानिवृत्तौ स्वातन्त्र्यलाभात् प्राक् व्याख्यातं यत् 'चित्तं' तदेव संकोचिनीं बहिर्मुखतां जहत्, 'अन्तर्मुखीभावेन चेतनपदाध्यारोहात्'—ग्राहकभूमिकाक्रमणक्रमेण संकोचकलाया अपि विगलनेन स्वरूपापत्त्या 'चितिर्' भवति; स्वां चिन्मयीं परां भूमिमाविशति इत्यर्थः ॥ १३ ॥

ननु यदि पारमार्थिकं चिच्छक्तिपदं सकलभेदकवलनस्वभावं, तत् अस्य

Commentary

From the point of view of the knowable object, this *sūtra* has been practically explained already in detail in connexion with the explanation of the previous *sūtra*. From the point of view of the wording, however, it is being explained now.

After full knowledge of *it* (i.e. of the self's authorship of the five-fold act), the cause, viz., the lack of knowledge being removed, the delusion caused by one's own *śakti* (power) having ceased, because of the attainment of *svātantrya* the *citta* (explained earlier in Sūtra 5) giving up the limiting tendency of extroversion, becoming introverted, rises to the status of *cetana*, that is, gradually it rises to the status of the knowing subject, where by the dissolution of the aspect of limitation, and attaining its real nature, it becomes *citi*. It now enters its highest stage of *cit*— this is the sense.

A question arises here,—If *cit-śakti* in its highest aspect is of such a nature as cancels (lit. devours) all difference§ it should remain so (i.e. it should retain that nature) even in

---

§ Prof. Leidecker reads *Sakala-bheda-kavalana-svabhāva* as Sakala-bheda-*kabalana*-svabhāva. and so has given a very incorrect translation of this passage.

मायापदेऽपि तथारूपेण भवितव्यं यथा जलदाच्छादितस्यापि भानोः भावावभासकत्वम् । इत्याशङ्क्य आह—

चितिवह्निरवरोहपदे छन्नोऽपि मात्रया
मेयेन्धनं प्लुष्यति ॥ १४ ॥

'चितिरेव' विश्वग्रसनशीलत्वात् 'वह्निः'; असौ एव 'अवरोहपदे'–मायाप्रमातृतायां 'छन्नोऽपि'–स्वातन्त्र्यात् आच्छादितस्वभावोऽपि, भूरिभूतिच्छन्नाग्निवत् 'मात्रया'–अंशेन, नीलपीतादिप्रमेयेन्धनं 'प्लुष्यति'–स्वात्मसात्-करोति । मात्रापदस्य इदम् आकूतम्–यत् कवलयन् अपि सार्वात्म्येन न ग्रसते,

the *māyā* — sphere (i.e. even in its condition of manifestation of the universe) just as the Sun manifests objects even when it is covered by clouds. (i.e. It is the nature of the Sun to manifest objects, and it does so even when it is covered by clouds. Even so if it is the nature of *citi* to cancel all difference, it should retain this nature even when it is covered by *māyā*. *Citi* is compared to the Sun, *māyā* is compared to clouds) Raising this doubt, the author replies below:

Sūtra 14. The fire of citi even when it descends to the (lower) stage, though covered (by māyā) partly burns the fuel of the known (objects).

Commentary

Citi is (here likened to) fire because it devours (i.e. assimilates to itself) the (phenomenal) universe. It in its stage of descent in the *māyā-pramātā* (i.e. experient conditioned by *māyā*), though covered (by *māyā*), because of its (inherent) freedom, partly burns i.e. assimilates to itself the fuel of the objects of knowledge such as blue, yellow etc., in spite of its true nature being veiled, even as fire burns the fuel though

अपि तु अंशेन; संस्कारात्मना उत्थापयति । ग्रासकत्वं च सर्वप्रमातॄणां स्वानुभवत एव सिद्धम् । यदुक्तं श्रीमदुत्पलदेवपादैः निजस्तोत्रेषु

'वर्तन्ते जन्तवोऽशेषा अपि ब्रह्मेन्द्रविष्णवः ।
ग्रसमानास्ततो वन्दे देव विश्वं भवन्मयम् ॥

इति ॥ १४ ॥

covered by copious ashes.* (The sense is that since the objects of knowledge are assimilated by consciousness to itself; their difference is annihilated. As *knowledge*, the objects are simply part and parcel of consciousness itself). The intention of using the word *mātrā* (in part, partly) (in the *sūtra*) is this — Though devouring (the object of knowledge), it does not consume it wholly, but only *partly*, because it again makes it rise by means of the *saṁskāras* (i.e. the impressions of the object left on the mind). That all experients have the power of devouring (i.e. assimilating objects of experience to consciousness) is proved by one's own experience. As has been (rightly) said by the revered Utpaladeva[134] in his hymns—

"Since all the creatures, even Brahmā, Indra, and Viṣṇu,[135] go on devouring (i.e. assimilating), therefore, O God, I adore the universe that is of your own form."§ (*Śiva-stotrāvali* xx. 17).

* *bhūti* here means ashes, not 'great power' as translated by Prof. Leidecker. The ashes are compared to *māyā*; *citi* is compared to 'fire'.

§ The idea is that all conscious beings go on devouring i.e. experiencing objects in various ways i.e assimilating things to themselves; therefore, I adore the universe which is simply yourself inasmuch as you constantly assimilate it to yourself.

Prof. Leidecker translates *grasamānāḥ* as 'are *being devoured*' which is even grammatically indefensible, to say nothing from the point of view of sense.

यदा पुनः करणेश्वरीप्रसरसंकोचं संपाद्य सर्गसंहारक्रमपरिशीलनयुक्तिम् आविशति तदा

बललाभे विश्वमात्मसात्करोति ॥ १५ ॥

चितिरेव देहप्राणाद्याच्छादननिमज्जनेन स्वरूपम् उन्मग्नत्वेन स्फारयन्ती बलम्; यथोक्तं

'तदाक्रम्य बलं मन्त्राः ··· ··· ।

इति । एवं च 'बललाभे'–उन्मग्नस्वरूपाश्रयणे क्षित्यादि-सदाशिवान्तं 'विश्वम् आत्मसात् करोति'–स्वस्वरूपाभेदेन निर्भासयति । तदुक्तं पूर्वगुरुभिः स्वभाषामयेषु क्रमसूत्रेषु

When, however, (the aspirant) by accomplishing the *prasara* or forth-going of the (divine) senses adopts the means of the practice of *sarga* or emanation (of the objective existence) and by accomplishing the *saṅkoca* or withdrawing (of the senses) adopts the means of the practice of *saṁhāra*, or withdrawal (of the objective existence) § then

Sūtra 15. In acquiring the (inherent) power, of citi, he, the aspirant assimilates the universe to himself.

Commentary

Citi by the submergence of the covering of body, *prāṇa*, etc. and by bringing into prominence her essential nature, by her emergence is, *bala* or power. As has been said,

Then having resorted to that power, the *mantras*[136] (acquire the power and efficiency of the all-knowing i.e. Śiva.)

Thus when the power (of consciousness) is gained i.e. when one betakes to one's real nature that has now emerged,

§ Here, *prasara* and *saṅkoca* of the senses are connected successively with *sarga* and *saṁhāra* of the objective existence. *Saṅkoca* in this context does not mean contraction or limitation, but closing, withdrawing.

'यथा वह्निरुद्बोधितो दाह्यं दहति, तथा विषयपाशान्
भक्षयेत्'

इति ।

'न चैवं वक्तव्यम्—विश्वात्मसात्काररूपा समावेशभूः कादाचित्की । कथम् उपादेया इयं स्यात् इति; यतो देहाद्युन्मज्जननिमज्जनवशेन इदम् अस्याः कादाचित्कत्वम् इव आभाति । वस्तुतस्तु चितिस्वातन्त्र्यावभासितदेहाद्युन्मज्जनात् एव कादाचित्कत्वम् । एषा तु सदैव प्रकाशमाना; अन्यथा तत् देहादि अपि न प्रकाशेत । अत एव देहादिप्रमातृताभिमाननिमज्जनाय

one makes the universe from the earth to Sadāśiva one's own i.e. makes the universe appear as identical with his Self. This has been said by the ancient teachers in the '*Kramasūtras*' in their own characteristic language—

Just as fire set ablaze consumes the fuel, even so should one consume the objects of sense which act like fetters".

It would not be right to say—"The* all-inclusive role of *citi* when it assimilates to itself the entire universe is only temporary. How then can it (i.e. the inclusive role) be accepted ?" (This objection is not valid), for the inclusive nature of *citi* appears as temporary only because of the emergence and immergence of the body etc. In reality, the temporary appearance of the inclusive nature of *citi* is due to the emergence of the body etc. which are brought into manifestation by the sovereign will of *citi* herself. This all-inclusive role, however, is ever in manifestation. Otherwise (i.e. if *citi* were not ever in manifestation), even the body etc. would not be manifested (i.e. would not appear as objects of consciousness).

---

*Prof. Leidecker's translation of this passage hardly makes any sense.

अभ्यासः, न तु सदा प्रथमानतासारप्रमातृता-
प्राप्त्यर्थम्,

इति श्रीप्रत्यभिज्ञाकाराः ॥ १५ ॥

एवं च

**चिदानन्दलाभे देहादिषु चेत्यमानेष्वपि चिदैकात्म्य-
प्रतिपत्तिदाढर्यं जीवन्मुक्तिः ॥ १६ ॥**

विश्वात्मसात्कारात्मनि समावेशरूपे 'चिदानन्दे लब्धे' व्युत्थानदशायां दलकल्पतया देहप्राणनीलसुखादिषु आभासमानेषु अपि, यत्समावेशसंस्कारबलात् प्रतिपादयिष्यमाणयुक्तिक्रमोपबृंहितात् 'चिदैकात्म्यप्रतिपत्तिदाढर्यम्'—अविचला,

Therefore the practice (the yogic practice) is recommended in order to remove the (false) identification of the experient with the body etc. not for attaining the status of the experiencing consciousness that by its very nature is always luminous.

This is what the author of the excellent *Pratyabhijñā* means.

And thus :

Sūtra 16. When the bliss of cit is attained, there is stability of the consciousness of identity with cit even while the body etc. are being experienced. This state is jīvanmukti (i.e. mukti even while one is alive).

Commentary

When on the attainment of the bliss of consciousness i.e. on the attainment of *samāveśa*[137] or contemplative experience of unity consciousness in which the entire universe is experienced as identical with the Self, even in *vyutthāna*[138] condition in which the body, *prāṇa*, blue, pleasure etc.[139] are experienced like so many coverings, there is firmness in the consciousness of identity with *cit* i.e. there is lasting experience of unity

चिदेकत्वप्रथा, सैव 'जीवन्मुक्तिः'-जीवतः प्राणान् अपि धारयतो मुक्तिः; प्रत्यभिज्ञातनिजस्वरूपविद्रावितशेषपाशराशित्वात् । यथोक्तं स्पन्दशास्त्रे

'इति वा यस्य संवित्तिः क्रीडात्वेनाखिलं जगत् ।
स पश्यन्सततं युक्तो जीवन्मुक्तो न संशयः ॥'

इति ॥ १६ ॥

अथ कथं चिदानन्दलाभो भवति ? इत्याह—

मध्यविकासाच्चिदानन्दलाभः ॥ १७ ॥

सर्वान्तरतमत्वेन वर्तमानत्वात् तद्भित्तिलग्नतां विना च कस्यचित् अपि

consciousness with *cit* on account of the force of the impressions (left behind) of the unity-consciousness (produced) during contemplation which is strengthened by the various means to be propounded, then that firmness of consciousness of identity with *cit* is *jīvanmukti*, i.e. liberation of one who is still alive i.e. who still retains his vital breaths, because in that condition there is complete dissolution of the fetters (of ignorance) on the recognition of one's true nature.

As has been said in the *Spandaśāstra*—

"He who knows thus (i.e. the universe is identical with the Self) and regards the whole world as a play, (of the Divine), being ever united (with the universal consciousness), is without doubt, liberated even while alive"

(*Spandakārikā*, Niṣyanda II, verse 5).

How is the bliss of *cit* acquired ? Regarding this the *Sūtrakāra* (the composer of the sūtras) says :

Sūtra 17. By the development of the madhya (centre) is there acquisition of the bliss of the cit.

The exalted *Saṁvit* (universal consciousness) itself is the centre inasmuch as it is present as the innermost (reality)

स्वरूपानुपपत्तेः संविदेव भगवती 'मध्यम्'। सा तु मायावशायां तथाभूतापि स्वरूपं गूहयित्वा

'प्राक् संवित्प्राणे परिणता'

इति नीत्या प्राणशक्तिभूमिं स्वीकृत्य, अवरोहक्रमेण बुद्धिदेहादिभुवम् अधिशयाना, नाडीसहस्रसरणिम् अनुसृता। तत्रापि च पलाशपर्णमध्यशाखान्यायेन आब्रह्मरन्ध्रात् अधोवक्त्रपर्यन्तं प्राणशक्तिब्रह्माश्रयमध्यमनाडीरूपतया प्राधान्येन स्थिता; तत एव सर्ववृत्तीनाम् उदयात्, तत्रैव च विश्रामात्। एवंभूतापि एषा पशूनां निमीलितस्वरूपैव स्थिता। यदा तु उक्तयुक्तिक्रमेण सर्वान्तरतमत्वे मध्यभूता संविद्भगवती विकसति, यदि वा वक्ष्यमाणक्रमेण मध्यभूता ब्रह्मनाडी विकसति, तदा 'तद्विकासात्

of all and inasmuch as the form or nature of any thing whatsoever cannot be possible without its being attached to it (i.e. *Saṁvit* or universal consciousness) as the ground or support. In spite of its being so (i.e. in spite of its being the innermost reality and ground of every possible thing), according to the dictum—"at first *samvit* is transformed into *prāṇa*", it conceals its real nature in the stage of *Māyā* and accepting the role of *prāṇa-śakti*,[140] resting in the planes of *buddhi*, body etc. in a descending order, it has followed the course of the thousand *nāḍis*. Even there (i.e. at the stage of the individual embodiment) it remains principally in the form of the *madhyama-nāḍī*[141] whose substratum is Brahman in the form of *prāṇa-śakti*, right from *brahmarandhra*[142] down to *adho vaktra*[143] like the central rib of a *palāśa*[144] leaf. (It is called *madhyama-nāḍī* or central *nāḍi*) because all the functions arise from that and come to rest there. Even though thus constituted, its nature remains hidden to the *paśus* (i.e. the ignorant *jīvas*). When, however, the exalted *samvit* (consciousness) which, being the innermost reality of all forms the centre (*madhya*), develops by the process of the

चिदानन्दस्य' उक्तरूपस्य 'लाभः'–प्राप्तिर्भवति । ततश्च प्रागुक्ता जीवन्मुक्तिः ॥ १७ ॥

मध्यविकासे युक्तिमाह

विकल्पक्षय-शक्तिसंकोचविकास-वाहच्छेदाद्यन्तकोटि-निभालनादय इहोपायाः ॥ १८ ॥

'इह मध्यशक्तिविकासे 'विकल्पक्षयादय उपायाः' । प्रागुपदिष्ट-पञ्चविधकृत्यकारित्वाद्यनुसरणेन सर्वमध्यभूतायाः संविदो विकासो जायते—इति अभिहितप्रायम् । उपायान्तरम् अपि तु उच्यते;—

means described above (i.e. by the practice[145] of *pañcakṛtya*) or when the central *brahma-nāḍī*[146] develops[147] as is to be described, then because of the development of that, there comes the attainment of the bliss of *cit* (the universal consciousness). Then comes liberation while one is alive as described before.

With reference to the method which brings about the development of the centre, it is said :

Sūtra 18. Herein the means are, dissolution of vikalpa, saṅkoca and vikāsa of śakti, cutting of the vāhas, the practice (of the contemplation) of the koṭi (point, extremity) of the beginning and the end etc.

Commentary

Herein i.e. in the unfolding of the central *śakti*, the dissolution of *vikalpa*, etc. are the means. It has already been explained that the unfoldment of *samvid* which forms the centre of all is achieved by following the authorship of the five-fold process as already taught. However, another means is also being mentioned. There is an easy means by which one can dispense with (lit. shatter) all the fetters of rigorous disciplines

प्राणायाम-मुद्राबन्धादिसमस्तयन्त्रणातन्त्रत्रोटनेन सुखोपायमेव, हृदये निहित-चित्तः, उक्तयुक्त्या स्वस्थितिप्रतिबन्धकं विकल्पम् अकिंचिच्चिन्तकत्वेन प्रशमयन्, अविकल्पपरामर्शेन देहाद्यकलुषस्वचित्प्रमातृतानिभालनप्रवणः, अचिरादेव उन्मिषद्विकासां तुर्यतुर्यातीतसमावेशदशाम् आसादयति। यथोक्तम्—

'विकल्पहानेनैकाग्र्यात्क्रमेणेश्वरतापदम्।'

like *prāṇāyāma*,[148] *mudrā*,[149] *bandha*[150] etc. When (an aspirant) keeps his *citta* (individual consciousness) concentrated on the *samvid* or *cit* (lit. heart)* restraining, by the method alluded to, the *vikalpas*[151] that obstruct staying in one's real nature, by not§ thinking of anything whatsoever. and thus by laying hold of *avikalpa* state, he becomes used to the habit of regarding his *cit* as the (real) knower, untarnished by body etc., and so within a short time only, he attains absorption into *turya*[152] and the state transcending *turya* (*turyātīta*)[153] which are on the point of unfolding.

As has been said in *Īśvara-pratyabhijñā*, (IV A.I. Ā, kā, 11) "By giving up *vikalpa*, and by one-pointedness (of mind), one gradually reaches the stage of Iśvara-ship.

**Hṛdaya* here does not mean the physical heart, but the deepest consciousness. It has been called *hṛdaya* or heart, because it is the centre of reality. It is the light of consciousness in which the entire universe is rooted. In the individual, it is the spiritual centre.

§Prof. Leidecker translates this in the following way : "by becoming liberated from all sorrow whatsoever, he is banishing *vikalpa* which impedes cheerfulness". How he has arrived at this interpretation passes all comprehension.

इति श्रीप्रत्यभिज्ञायाम् । श्रीस्पन्देऽपि

'यदा क्षोभः प्रलीयेत तदा स्यात्परमं पदम् ॥'

इति । श्रीज्ञागर्भेऽपि

'विहाय सकलाः क्रिया जननि मानसीः सर्वतो
विमुक्तकरणक्रियानुसृतिपारतन्त्र्योज्ज्वलम् ।
स्थितैस्त्वदनुभावतः सपदि वेद्यते सा परा
दशा नृभिरतन्द्रितासमसुखामृतस्यन्दिनी ॥'

इति । अयं च उपायो मूर्धन्यत्वात् प्रत्यभिज्ञायां प्रतिपादितत्वात् आदौ उक्तः । शक्तिसंकोचादयस्तु यद्यपि प्रत्यभिज्ञायां न प्रतिपादिताः, तथापि आम्नायिकत्वात् अस्माभिः प्रसङ्गात् प्रदर्श्यन्ते; बहुषु हि प्रदर्शितेषु कश्चित् केनचित् प्रवेक्ष्यति इति ।

In excellent *Spanda* also (it has been said) :

"When, (mental) agitation would dissolve, then would ensue the highest stage".

—*Spandakārika*, Ni. I, kā. 9

So also in *Jñānagarbha*, (it has been said) :

"When, O mother, men renounce all mental activities and are poised in a pure state being free from the bondage of the pursuit of sense-activities, then by thy grace is that supreme state realized at once which rains down the nectar of undiminished and unparalleled happiness."*

This means has been described first, because it is the highest and because it has been taught in the *Pratybhijñā* doctrine. The *saṅkoca* of śakti etc , though not taught in the *Pratyabhijñā* doctrine, have been, nevertheless, mentioned by us on account of their belonging to the sacred tradition and their

* *Vimukta-karaṇa-kriyānusṛti-pārtantryojjvalam* has been translated by Prof. Leidecker as "their dependence ends in flames, because they devote themselves to the activity of the organ of those that are saved." This is a deplorable sample of many such meaningless translations with which the book is replete.

'शक्तेः संकोच'—इन्द्रियद्वारेण प्रसरन्त्या एव आकुञ्चनक्रमेण उन्मुखीकरणम् । यथोक्तम् आथर्वणिकोपनिषत्सु कठवल्ल्यां चतुर्थवल्लीप्रथममन्त्रे ।

'पराञ्चि खानि व्यतृणत्स्वयंभू-
स्तस्मात्पराङ्पश्यति नान्तरात्मन् ।
कश्चिद्धीरः प्रत्यगात्मानमैक्षद्
आवृत्तचक्षुरमृतत्वमश्नन् ॥'

इति । प्रसृताया अपि वा कूर्माङ्गसंकोचवत् त्रासमये हृत्प्रवेशयञ्च सर्वतो निवर्तनम् । यथोक्तम्

'तदपोद्धृते नित्योदितस्थितिः ।'

इति ।

incidental connexion with it. If many means are described, some one may enter (the state of *samāveśa*) through any one of them. The *saṅkoca* of Śakti means turning in towards the Self, by the process of withdrawal, of that consciousness which is spreading externally through the gates of the senses (towards the objects). As has been said in the first *mantra* of the 4th chapter of Kaṭhavallī belonging to the *Atharva upaniṣads*.[154]

> **The self-existent one pierced the openings (of the senses) outward**
> **Hence one looks outward, not within one's Self**
> **Some wise man, wishing to taste immortality**
> **With reverted eyes (i.e. introspectively)**
> **beholds (lit. beheld) the immanent Self.**

or (the *saṅkoca* of the *śakti* may be) the (sudden) turning back from all sides of the externally spread *śakti* like the contraction of the limbs of the tortoise and its withdrawal into the interior on the occasion of fear. As has been said, "It being

'शक्तेर्विकासः, अन्तर्निगूढाया अक्रममेव सकलकरणचक्र-विस्फारणेन

'अन्तर्लक्ष्यो बहिर्दृष्टिर्निमेषोन्मेषवर्जितः ।'

इति । भैरवीयमुद्रानुप्रवेशयुक्त्या बहिः प्रसरणम् । यथोक्तं कक्ष्यास्तोत्रे

'सर्वाः शक्तीश्चेतसा दर्शनाद्याः
स्वे स्वे वेद्ये यौगपद्येन विष्वक् ।
क्षिप्त्वा मध्ये हाटकस्तम्भभूत-
स्तिष्ठन्विश्वाधार एकोऽवभासि ॥'

इति । श्रीभट्टकल्लटेनापि उक्तम्

'रूपादिषु परिणामात् तत्सिद्धिः ।'

reverted there is resting in the ever-present (ātman).[155] The *vikāsa* of *Śakti* hidden within results from the simultaneous opening of all the sense-organs.

"The object (of one's aspiration) is to be seen within, while the external sight may be kept steady without closing and opening of the eye-lids."

This technique of inner absorption with external expansion of the senses is known as *bhairavīmudrā.*

As has been said in *Kakṣyāstotra*—

"Throwing by will all the powers like seeing etc. simultaneously and on all sides into their respective objects and remaining (unmoved) *within* like a gold pillar, you (O Śiva) alone appear as the foundation of the universe".

Kallaṭa, the great scholar has also said, "That (i.e. the development or *vikāsa* of *madhya śakti*) is accomplished by transformation (i.e. by viewing the consciousness that considers itself as outgoing as the same that is inward) even in the

इति शक्तेश्च संकोचविकासौ, नासापुटस्पन्दनक्रमोन्मिषत्सूक्ष्मप्राणशक्त्या भ्रूभेदनेन क्रमासादितोर्ध्वकुण्डलिनीपदे प्रसरविश्रान्ति-दशापरिशीलनम्; अधःकुण्डलिन्यां च षष्ठवक्त्ररूपायां प्रगुणीकृत्य शक्तिं, तन्मूल-तदग्र-तन्मध्यभूमिस्पर्शावेशः । यथोक्तं विज्ञानभट्टारके

'वह्नेर्विषस्य मध्ये तु चित्तं सुखमयं क्षिपेत् ।
केवलं वायुपूर्णं वा स्मरानन्देन युज्यते ॥'

इति । अत्र वह्निः अनुप्रवेशक्रमेण संकोचभूः, विषस्थानम् प्रसरयुक्त्या विकासपदम्, 'विष्लृ व्याप्तौ' इति अर्थानुगमात् ।

presence of forms* etc." So far as *saṅkoca* and *vikāsa* of Śakti are concerned, *vikāsa* connotes the practice of the condition of expansion and resting of *śakti* in the stage of the *ūrdhva-kuṇḍalini*[156] gradually brought about by the restraint of the *prāṇa* between the eye-brows which (restraint) is accomplished by the power of the subtle *prāṇa* which develops gradually through the regulation of the vibrations in the cavities of the nose.

In the state of *adhaḥ kuṇḍalini*[157] whose location is indicated by the sixth organ of *meḍhrakanda*[158] after strengthening the *prāṇa śakti*, there is entrance or absorption in its root, tip and middle. As has been said in Vijñāna-bhaṭṭāraka

"One should throw (i.e. concentrate) the delightful *citta* in the middle of *vahni* and *viṣa*[159] whether by itself or permeated by *vāyu* (prāṇic breath) one would then be joined to the bliss of sexual union (smarānanda).[160]

—*Vijñānabhairava*, 68

Here *vahni* represents the stage of *saṅkoca* by the process of the entrance of *prāṇa* (in *meḍhra-kanda*). The *viṣa* locus represents the stage of *vikāsa*, by the technique of *prasara* in

---

* Prof. Leidecker translates *rūpādiṣu pariṇāmāt* as 'owing to the change in form — which is incorrect. The development of *madhya-śakti* is accomplished not by change in form but by the transformation of consciousness.

'वाहयोः'—वामदक्षिणगतयोः प्राणापानयोः 'छेदो'—हृदय-विश्रान्ति-पुरःसरम् अन्तः ककारहकारादिप्रायानच्कवर्णोच्चारेण विच्छेदनम् । यथोक्तं ज्ञानगर्भे

'अनच्ककक्कृतायतिप्रसृतपार्श्वनाडीद्वय-
च्छिदो विधृतचेतसो हृदयपङ्कजस्योदरे ।
उदेति तव दारितान्धतमसः स विद्याङ्कुरो
य एष परमेशतां जनयितुं पशोरप्यलम् ।।

इति ।

'आदिकोटिः' हृदयम्, 'अन्तकोटिः' द्वादशान्तः; तयोः प्राणोल्लास-

accordance with the etymological explanation of the root *viṣ* to pervade.[161]*

By both *vāhas* is to be understood *prāṇa* and *apāna* of which one (viz. *apāna*) is concerned with the right and the other (viz. *prāna*) is concerned with the left (*nāḍī* or channel of *vāyu*); *cheda* means cessation or pause by the sounding of *anacka*[162] sounds like *ka*, *ha* etc. inwardly before which, however, they should be stopped in the heart. As has been said in *Jñāna-garbha*:

"In the heart-lotus of one whose mind has been controlled, whose two *nāḍis* (the channels of *vāyu*) (i.e. whose flow of *vāyu* in the two *nāḍis*) extending on both sides have been stilled by the restraint brought about by sounding vowel-less 'K' and whose blinding darkness has been dispelled, arises that sprout of your knowledge, O, (world mother) which is adequate to produce *parameśaship* even in the *paśu*".[163]

The first point is the heart. The last point is the measure

* This is highly mystic. See the notes 156-161 for exposition. Prof. Leidecker's translation of this passage is simply hopeless. It is impossible to work away the translation of such passages without understanding their import from a teacher who is initiated in the tradition of the school.

विश्रान्त्यवसरे 'निभालनं'—चित्तनिवेशनेन परिशीलनम् । यथोक्तं विज्ञानभैरवे

'हृद्याकाशे निलीनाक्षः पद्मसंपुटमध्यगः ।
अनन्यचेताः सुभगे परं सौभाग्यमाप्नुयात् ॥'

इति । तथा

'यथा तथा यत्र तत्र द्वादशान्ते मनः क्षिपेत् ।
प्रतिक्षणं क्षीणवृत्तेर्वैलक्षण्यं दिनैर्भवेत् ॥'

इति । आदिपदात् उन्मेषदशानिषेवणम् । यथोक्तम्

'उन्मेषः स तु विज्ञेयः स्वयं तमुपलक्षयेत् ॥'

इति स्पन्दे । तथा रमणीयविषयचर्वणादयश्च संगृहीताः । यथोक्तं श्रीविज्ञानभैरवे एव

of the twelve (a measure of twelve fingers).[164] *Nibhālana* means exercise or practice by fixing the mind at the time of the rising of prāṇa and its coming to an end between these two[165] (i.e between *hṛdaya* and *dvādaśānta*). As has been said in *Vijñāna-bhairava* (49th verse):

"He whose senses are merged (nilīnākṣaḥ) in the ether of the heart, who has entered mentally into the centre of the heart-lotus, who excludes every thing else from consciousness (i.e. who is one-pointed), attains to supreme happiness. O Beautiful one".[166]

So also has it been said in *Vijñānabhairava*, (51st verse):

"if one turns one's mind to *dvādaśānta* howsoever and wheresoever. the fluctuation of his mind will diminish every moment, and in a few days, he will acquire an extra-ordinary status."

The word *ādi* i.e. et cetera refers to the practice of *unmeṣa* condition. As has been said in the *Spanda* (*Spandakārikā* N. 3, Kā. 9).

That is to be known as *unmeṣa*;[167] one may see it for oneself".

'जग्धिपानकृतोल्लासरसानन्दविजृम्भणात् ।
भावयेद्भरितावस्थां महानन्दमयो भवेत् ।।
गीतादिविषयास्वादासमसौख्यैकतात्मनः ।
योगिनस्तन्मयत्वेन मनोरूढेस्तदात्मता ।
यत्र यत्र मनस्तुष्टिर्मनस्तत्रैव धारयेत् ।
तत्र तत्र परानन्दस्वरूपं संप्रकाशते ।।'

इति । एवमन्यदपि आनन्दपूर्णस्वात्मभावनादिकम् अनुमन्तव्यम् । इत्येवमादयः अत्र मध्यविकासे उपायाः ।। १८ ।।

मध्यविकासाच्चिदानन्दलाभः, स एव च परमयोगिनः समावेशसमा-

Under this concept are also summed up the tasting etc. of pleasant objects. As is said in the excellent *Vijñānabhairava* (72, 73, and 74 verses).

"When one experiences the expansion of the joy of savour arising from the pleasure of eating and drinking, one should meditate on the perfect condition of this joy, and then one would become full of great bliss.

When a *yogin* mentally becomes one with the incomparable joy of song and other objects, then of such a concentrated *yogin*, there is identity with that (i.e. with the incomparable joy), because he becomes one with it.

Wherever the *manas* (the individual mind) finds its satisfaction, let it be concentrated on that. In every such case, the true nature of the highest bliss will shine forth.[168]

So also any other *bhāvanā* (meditation) on the Self full of bliss may be inferred. The word, 'et cetera' in the *sūtra* refers to such methods for the development of the *madhya* (centre).

From the development of the *madhya* results the attainment of the bliss of the spirit. This (attainment of the bliss of the spirit) indeed is the *samādhi* (at-one-ment) of the highest

पत्यादिपर्यायः समाधिः, तस्य नित्योदितत्वे युक्तिमाह—

समाधिसंस्कारवति व्युत्थाने भूयो भूयश्चिदैक्या-
मर्शान्नित्योदितसमाधिलाभः ॥ १६ ॥

आसादितसमावेशो योगिवरो व्युत्थाने अपि समाधिरससंस्कारेण क्षीव इव सानन्दं घूर्णमानो, भावराशिं शरदभ्रलवम् इव चिद्गगन एव लीयमानं पश्यन्, भूयो भूयः अन्तर्मुखताम् एव समवलम्बमानो, निमीलनसमाधिक्रमेण चिदैक्यमेव विमृशन् व्युत्थानाभिमतावसरे अपि समाध्येकरस एव भवति । यथोक्तं क्रमसूत्रेषु

yogin, known also as *Samāveśa*,[169] *samāpatti* and other such synonymous terms. For bringing about its permanence (i.e. the permanence of *Samādhi*), the (following) method has been mentioned.

Sūtra 19. In vyutthāna which is full of the after-effects of samādhi, there is the attainment of permanent samādhi by dwelling on one's identity with cit (the universal, supreme consciousness) over and over again.

Commentary

A great Yogin who has attained to *Samāveśa*, is still full of the *samādhi*-state even on the occasion of what is considered to be *vyutthāna*,[170] beholding as he does, even in the condition of *vyutthāna*, the (entire) mass of entities to be dissolving in the *cit-sky* like a bit of cloud in autumn,* reeling joyfully owing to the (persisting) after-effect of the savour of *samādhi*, like one intoxicated, resorting to introversion again and again, and meditating on his identity with *cit* by the process of *nimīlana-samādhi*.[171] As has been said in the *Krama-sūtras* "The

* This state appears when *dehātma-bhāva* or the delusion of identity with the body disappears.

'क्रममुद्रया अन्तःस्वरूपया बहिर्मुखः समाविष्टो भवति साधकः। तत्रादौ बाह्यात् अन्तः प्रवेशः, आभ्यन्तरात् बाह्यस्वरूपे प्रवेशः आवेशवशात् जायते;—इति सबाह्याभ्यन्तरोऽयं मुद्राक्रमः'

इति। अत्रायमर्थः सृष्टि-स्थिति-संहृतिसंविच्चक्रात्मकं क्रमं मुद्रयति, स्वाधिष्ठितम् आत्मसात् करोति येयं तुरीया चितिशक्तिः, तया 'क्रममुद्रया'; 'अन्तरिति'—पूर्णाहन्तास्वरूपया; 'बहिर्मुख'—इति, विषयेषु व्यापृतः अपि; 'समाविष्टः'—साक्षात्कृतपरशक्तिस्फारः 'साधकः'—परमयोगी भवति। तत्र च 'बाह्याद्' ग्रस्यमानात् विषयग्रामात् 'अन्तः'

sādhaka (the aspirant practising yogic discipline), (even) while gazing outward remains in *samāveśa* by *Kramā mudrā*[172] which is characterized by inwardness. Owing to the force of *āveśa*, there takes place in this, first an entrance of consciousness from the external into the internal, and (then) from the internal into the external. Thus this *mudrā-krama* is both of the nature of the external and internal." This is the meaning of this quotation. *Krama-mudrayā* i.e. by *krama-mudrā*. *Krama* means the succession of the cyclic consciousness of emanation (*sṛṣṭi*), maintenance (*sthiti*), and re-absorption (*saṁhṛti*). *Mudrā* means *mudrayati* i.e. the *turiyā* (fourth) power of consciousness (consciously) makes one's own the world-process which (already) rests in one's (highest) Self. (So the whole thing means) — By *krama-mudrā* i.e. by that *turiyā* power of universal consciousness which (consciously) assimilates to one self the succession of emanation, maintenance and re-absorption which (already) rests in the (highest) Self. *Antaḥ-svarūpayā* means by the essential nature of the full or perfect 'I'. (The entire sentence means) — The *sādhaka* i.e. the aspirant, the yogin of the highest type becomes *samāviṣṭa* i.e. one who has realized the unfolding of the highest *Śakti* even while he is extroverted i.e. even while he is busying himself with sense-objects. (This he is able to do) by '*Krama-*

परस्यां चितिभूमौ, ग्रसनक्रमेणैव 'प्रवेशः'—समावेशो भवति । 'आभ्यन्तरात्' चितिशक्तिस्वरूपात् च साक्षात्कृतात् 'आवेशवशात्'—समावेशसामर्थ्यात् एव 'बाह्यस्वरूपे'—इदन्तानिर्भासे विषयग्रामे, वमनयुक्त्या 'प्रवेशः'—चिद्रसाश्यानताप्रथनात्मा समावेशो जायते;—इति 'सबाह्याभ्यन्तरः अयं' नित्योदितसमावेशात्मा 'मुदो'—हर्षस्य वितरणात्, परमानंद-स्वरूपत्वात्, पाशद्रावणात्, विश्वस्य अन्तः तुरीयसत्तायां मुद्रणात् च मुद्रात्मा,

mudrā which is of the nature of full consciousness of the perfect self. In this process, there occurs, through the assimilation (lit. devouring) of the totality of the external sense-objects into the internal i.e. into the highest *citi* plane (the plane of highest or universal consciousness), penetration into the inner or *samāveśa* by the very process of assimilation. Again there occurs, through the internal i.e. through the realization of the nature of *citiśakti* by the power of *samāveśa*, a penetration or entrance into the external i.e. into the totality of sense-objects appearing as the this (*idantā*) by the process of externalization (*vamana*). This (*praveśa* or penetration or entrance) is (also) a *samāveśa* of the nature of the manifestation of the solidification of the essence of *cit* (universal consciousness).

His eternally active (*nityodita*) *samāveśa*, which is external and internal at the same time, is of the nature of *mudrā*,* because :

(1) It distributes *muda* i.e. joy on account of its being

---

* Mudrā is etymologically derived in three ways : *mudam rāti* (*dadāti*) i.e. that which gives *mud* or joy (2) *mum drāvayati* i.e. that which dissolves *mu* (bondage), (3) *mudrayati iti* i.e. that which seals up [the universe into *turīya*].

क्रमः अपि सृष्ट्यादिक्रमाभासकत्वात् तत्क्रमाभासरूपत्वात् च 'क्रम' इति अभिधीयते इति ॥ १९ ॥

इदानीम् अस्य समाधिलाभस्य फलमाह

तदा प्रकाशानन्दसारमहामन्त्रवीर्यात्मकपूर्णाहन्तावेशात्सदा सर्वसर्गसंहारकारिनिजसंविद्देवताचक्रेश्वरताप्राप्ति-र्भवतीति शिवम् ॥ २० ॥

नित्योदिते समाधौ लब्धे सति, 'प्रकाशानन्दसारा'—चिदाह्लादैकघना

of the nature of the highest bliss; (2) it dissolves (*drāvaṇāt*) all fetters; (3) it seals up the universe into the being of the inner *turīya* (the fourth or highest consciousness).

It is also called Krama (succession, cycle), because (1) it causes emanation *et cetera* to appear in succession (*krama*) (2) it itself consists in their successive appearance (*krama*).

Now he describes the fruit of the attainment of this *samādhi*.

Sūtra 20. Then (i.e. on the attainment of krama-mudrâ) as a result of entering into the perfect I-consciousness or Self which is in essence cit and ānanda (consciousness and bliss) and of the nature of the power of great mantra, there accrues the attainment of lordship over one's group of the deities of consciousness that brings about all emanation and re-absorption of the universe. All this is the nature of Śiva.

On attaining lasting *samādhi*, there accrues lordship over the group of the deities of consciousness[173] which (*cakra* or group) always brings about every kind of emanation and re-

'महती मन्त्रवीर्यात्मिका'—सर्वमन्त्रजीवितभूता 'पूर्णा' पराभट्टारिकारूपा या इयम् 'अहन्ता'—अकृत्रिमः स्वात्मचमत्कारः, तत्र 'आवेशात्' 'सदा' कालाग्न्यादेः चरमकलापर्यन्तस्य विश्वस्य यौ 'सर्गसंहारौ'—विचित्रौ सृष्टिप्रलयौ 'तत्कारि' यत् 'निजं संविद्देवताचक्रं' 'तदैश्वर्यस्य' 'प्राप्तिः'—आसादनं 'भवति' प्राकरणिकस्य परमयोगिन इत्यर्थः; 'इति' एतत् सर्वं शिवस्वरूपमेव इति उपसंहारः—इति संगतिः। तत्र यावत् इदं किंचित् संवेद्यते, तस्य संवेदनमेव स्वरूपं; तस्यापि अन्तर्मुखविमर्शमयाः प्रमातारः तत्त्वम्; तेषामपि विगलितदेहाद्युपाधिसंकोचाभिमाना अशेषशरीरा सदाशिवेश्वरतैव सारम्; अस्या अपि प्रकाशैकसद्भावापादिताशेषविश्वचमत्कारमयः श्रीमान् महेश्वर

absorption of the universe beginning with *Kālāgni*,[174] and ending with the last *Kalā* (phase) (known as *śāntā kalā*), by entering into the natural *camatkāra* or bliss of Self-consciousness which is of the essence of *prakāśa* and *ānanda* i.e. sheer compact consciousness and bliss, which is the very soul of all the mantras (*sarvamantra-jīvita-bhūtā*), which is perfect (*pūrṇā*) i.e. the highest *vimarśa* (*parābhaṭṭārikā-rūpā*).[175] This lordship accrues to the greatest Yogin referred to in this context. This is the meaning. *Iti Śivam* is to be construed as—'all this is (really) the form of Śiva—this is the conclusion. This being so, (it is to be understood that) the essence of whatever is cognised (i.e. *prameya*) is cognition (i.e. *pramāṇa*). Of this again, the inwardly turned experients (i.e. *pramātās*) full of self-consciousness are the essential truth.

Of these (experients) too, *sadāśiva-iśvaraship* is the essence in which the sense of identification with the limiting adjuncts of body *et cetera* has dissolved and whose body is the whole universe. And the highest reality of this (*Sadāśiva-īśvaraship*) is the blissful great Lord Himself who is full of *camatkāra*[176] or *vimarśa* (the bliss of perfect self-consciousness) of the entire

एव परमार्थः;—नहि पारमार्थिक-प्रकाशावेशं विना कस्यापि प्रकाशमानता घटते—स च परमेश्वरः स्वातन्त्र्यसारत्वात् आदि-क्षान्तामायीयशब्दराशि-परामर्शमयत्वेनैव एतत्स्वीकृतसमस्तवाच्य-वाचकमयाशेषजगदानन्दसद्भावा-पादनात् परं परिपूर्णत्वात् सर्वाकाङ्क्षाशून्यतया आनन्दप्रसरनिर्भरः; अत एव अनुत्तराकुलस्वरूपात् अकारात् आरभ्य शक्तिस्फाररूपहकलापर्यन्तं यत् विश्वं प्रसृतं, क्षकारस्य प्रसरशमनरूपत्वात्; तत् अकार-हकाराभ्यामेव

universe brought about by one-ness of being* (*eka-sadbhāva*) with *prakāśa* (the substratum of all manifestation).[177]

There cannot indeed be the manifestation of anything unless it shares (lit. enters) the light (the source and substratum of all manifestation) of the Highest Reality. And the Highest Lord is full of the flow of bliss, because of His being free from all desire, because of His being fully perfect, because of His being the essence of absolute freedom, and because of His having attained to the state of full *jagadānanda*[178] in having made his own the entire world consisting of indicator or word (*vācaka*) and indicated or object (*vācya*) by reflection (lit. seizing mentally) on the entire assemblage of *non-māyīya*† words[179] from '*a*' to '*kṣa*'.

Therefore the extended universe beginning with (the letter) '*a*' which is the nature of the highest '*akula*'[180] and upto the letter '*ha*' indicative of the unfolding or expansion of *Śakti*—'*kṣa*' indicating only the *finis* of the expansion—that (universe) flashing forth or vibrating, by virtue of the combination of '*a*' and '*ha*' and being accepted inwardly in

---

* *eka-sad-bhāva* means one-ness of being with (*prakāśa*), not the 'only reality (the existence)' as Prof. Leidecker thinks.

† Though the text even as accepted by Prof. Leidecker is क्षान्तामायीय शब्दराशि i.e. क्षान्त+अमायीय शब्दराशि, curiously enough he translates this as the "whole throng of *māyā*-sounds from '*a*' to '*kṣa*'.

संपुटीकारयुक्त्या प्रत्याहारन्यायेन अन्तः स्वीकृतं सत् अविभागवेदनात्मक-बिन्दुरूपतया स्फुरितम् अनुत्तर एव विश्राम्यति;—इति शब्दराशिस्वरूप एव अयम् अकृतको विमर्शः। यथोक्तं

'प्रकाशस्यात्मविश्रान्तिरहंभावो हि कीर्तितः।
उक्ता च सैव विश्रान्तिः सर्वापेक्षानिरोधतः॥
स्वातन्त्र्यमथ कर्तृत्वं मुख्यमीश्वरतापि च।'

इति। एवंच च अहन्ता सर्वमन्त्राणाम् उदयविश्रान्तिस्थानत्वात् एतद्बलेनैव च तत्तदर्थक्रियाकारित्वात् महती वीर्यभूमिः। तदुक्तम्

'तदाक्रम्य बलं मन्त्राः ... ...।'

इत्यादि

... ... त एते शिवधर्मिणः॥'

the manner of *pratyāhāra*[181] rests in the Highest Reality in the form of *bindu*[182] indicative of the consciousness of non-differentiation. Thus this natural *vimarśa* or inward experience is of the nature of the congregation of words.

As has been said (by Utpaladeva in *Ajaḍa-pramātṛ-siddhi*, verses 22-23).

"Resting of all objective experience† within oneself is what is meant by I-feeling. This 'resting' (within oneself), is called Sovereignty of Will, primary doership, and lordship because of the cancellation of all relational consciousness, and of dependence on anything outside oneself.‡

---

† *Prakāśa* here does not mean, the 'divine light'., but '*ghaṭasukhādi-vedya-prakśasya*'—all objective experience like jar, pleasure etc.

‡ "*Sarvāpekṣā-nirodhataḥ*" does not mean 'because 'perception of the universe is impeded', as Prof. Leidecker thinks.

इत्यन्तम् श्रीस्पन्दे । शिवसूत्रेषु अपि

'महाह्लदानुसंधानान्मन्त्रवीर्यानुभवः'उ० (१२२ सू०)

इति । तदत्र महामन्त्रवीर्यात्मिकायां पूर्णाहन्तायाम् 'आवेशो'—देहप्राणादि-निमज्जनात् तत्पदावाप्त्यवष्टम्भेन देहादीनां नीलादीनामपि तद्रसाप्लावनेन तन्मयीकरणम् । तथा हि—देहसुखनीलादि यत् किंचित् प्रथते, अध्यवसीयते, स्मर्यते, संकल्प्यते वा, तत्र सर्वत्रैव भगवती चितिशक्तिमयी प्रथा भित्तिभूतैव

This I-feeling is the stage of great power, for all *mantras* arise from and come to rest in it, and by its power all activities with an object are performed.

It has been said in the excellent *Spanda*, beginning with (i.e. *Spandakārikā*, Niṣyanda II, vv. 1-2)

"All *mantras* approaching this power" etc. and closing with

"All these (mantras) are endowed with the nature or the characteristic mark of Śiva."†

In *Śiva sūtras* also, it is said :

"By unification with the great lake,[183] one acquires the experience of *mantra* power."

Here, (i.e. in this *sūtra*) the penetration into the perfect Self which is of the nature of great *mantra*-power, is becoming one with it by the immersion of the body, *prāṇa* etc. (into it), by steadiness in the achievement of that stage (of perfect Self), and by immersing in its essence the (experience of) body, blue etc. So that then whatever appears e.g., the body, pleasure

† Here again Prof. Leidecker has bungled. '*Ta ete*' refers to the *mantras*. *Śivadharmiṇah* means '*Śivasya dharmaḥ* [*svabhāvaḥ*] [*asti*] *yeṣām te*" i.e. having the nature or characteristic mark of Śiva. This does not mean 'those who walk in the law of Śiva' as Prof. Leidecker thinks.

Cf. "मन्त्रा वर्णात्मकाः सर्वे, सर्वे वर्णाः शिवात्मकाः"—quoted by Kṣemarāja in his commentary on *Sūtra*-12.

स्फुरति;—तदस्फुरणे कस्यापि अस्फुरणात् इति उक्तत्वात्। केवलं तथा स्फुरन्त्यपि सा तन्मायाशक्त्या अवभासितदेहनीलाद्युपरागदत्ताभिमानवशात् भिन्न-भिन्नस्वभावा इव भान्ती ज्ञानसंकल्पाध्यवसायादिरूपतया मायाप्रमातृभिः अभिमन्यते; वस्तुतस्तु एकैव असौ चितिशक्तिः। यथोक्तम्—

"या चैषा प्रतिभा तत्तत्पदार्थक्रमरूषिता।
अक्रमानन्तचिद्रूपः प्रमाता स महेश्वरः ॥"

इति। तथा

(inner experience), blue (experience of outer objects) etc., or whatever is known for certain (by *Buddhi*) or remembered, or thought out (by *manas*)—in all these cases it is the play of *citi-śakti* which flashes forth as the background (of all experience). It has been (rightly) said, "without its flashing, there is no flashing of anything (whatever)." Only while flashing in this manner, she by *māyā-śakti* appearing as of this or that nature owing to her assuming the nature (lit. colour) of manifested body, blue etc., (i.e. owing to her considering herself as the body, blue, etc.), is considered by the *māyā*-subjects (i.e. *jīvas* or empirical selves) as knowledge, ideation, resolution etc. In reality, however, this *citi-śakti* is one and the same. As has been said (in *Īśvarapratyabhijñā*, Jñānādhikāra, VII Āhn. verse 1).

"That consciousness which is coloured (identified) with the succession of different objects (*tat-tat-padārthakrama*) is nothing other than the great Lord, the highest knower and of the nature of successionless* infinite consciousness."

So (also) (it has been said in *Īśvarapratyabhijñā*, Jñānādhikāra, V Āhn. verse 18).

* Maheśvara would be limited by time, if there is succession in His consciousness. His consciousness is *akrama* (timeless), *ananta* (spaceless).

'मायाशक्त्या विभोः सैव भिन्नसंवेद्यगोचरा ।
कथिता ज्ञानसंकल्पाध्यवसायादिनामभिः ॥'

इति । एवम् एषा सर्वदशासु एकैव चितिशक्तिः विजृम्भमाणा यदि तदनुप्रवेश-तदवष्टम्भयुक्त्या समासाद्यते, तत् तदावेशात् पूर्वोक्तयुक्त्या करणोन्मीलननिमीलनक्रमेण सर्वस्य सर्वमयत्वात् तत्तत्संहारादौ अपि 'सदा सर्वसर्गसंहारकारि' यत् 'सहजसंवित्तिदेवताचक्रम्'—अमायीयान्तर्बहिष्करण-मरीचिपुञ्जः, तत्र 'ईश्वरता'—साम्राज्यं परभैरवात्मता, तत्प्राप्तिः भवति परमयोगिनः । यथोक्तम्—

'यदा त्वेकत्र संरूढस्तदा तस्य लयोद्भवौ ।
नियच्छन्भोक्तृतामेति ततश्चक्रेश्वरो भवेत् ॥

"Owing to the *māyā śakti* of the Lord, she herself having to do with different knowables is called knowledge, ideation, resolution and by other names."

Thus it is one and the same *citi-śakti* which appears in various ways in all conditions. If by means of entry into and firm grip of her, she is attained (as described in *sūtra* 18), then by entering into her, and by the means previously described, i.e. by successive unfolding and infolding of the senses, because of everything being of the nature of everything else, even in the re-absorption etc. of every thing, whatever group of natural consciousness-deities there is, e.g. the non-*māyīyā* group of inner and external senses, which is ever projecting and ever withdrawing over all this the highest *yogin* acquires lordship and *parabhairava*-ship (i.e. becomes the highest *bhairava*).

As has been said

"When one is rooted in the one place i.e. into the *Spandatattva* consisting of the perfect I-consciousness, then controlling the *udbhava* (emanation) and *laya* (absorption) of it (i.e. of the *puryaṣṭaka* or *Sūkṣmaśarīra*—the subtle body and thereby of the universe also by means of *unmīlana* and *nimīlana samāveśa*), one acquires the status of a (real) enjoyer, and then becomes the lord of *cakra* (i.e. of the group of the sense-deities)".

—*Spandakārikā*, Niṣyanda III, 19

इति । अत्र एकत्र इति

'एकत्रारोपयेत्सर्वम्··· ···।'

इति चित्सामान्यस्पन्दभूः उन्मेषात्मा व्याख्यातव्या । तस्य इति अनेन

'पुर्यष्टकेन संरुद्ध··· ···।'

इति उपक्रान्तं पुर्यष्टकम् एव परामृष्टव्यम्; न तु यथा विवरणकृतः 'एकत्र सूक्ष्मे स्थूले शरीरे वा' इति व्याकृतवन्तः । स्तुतं च मया

Here 'the one place' (is explained in the following, *Spandakārikā*, Niṣyanda III. 12)

"Every thing should be deposited into the one place (i.e. into the *cit-śakti*)".

(Here) "*Ekatra*" or 'one place' should be interpreted as the state of the general vibration of *cit*, being of the nature of *unmeṣa*.

Then the word '*tasya*'* (its) in the verse cited above is to be understood to mean '*puryaṣṭaka*' (subtle body) inasmuch as the previous *Sūtra* (in *Spanda Kārikā* III. 17) begins with 'held or bound by *puryaṣṭaka* (subtle body)"§ It is not to be interpreted as 'in one place i.e. gross or subtle body', as Kallaṭācārya,† the author of *Vivaraṇa* has done.

---

* *Tasya*' (of it) as interpreted by the text refers to '*puryaṣṭaka*' or the subtle body, but a better interpretation as given by Svāmī Lakṣmaṇa Joo is that it refers to *śakti-cakra* or the group of *śaktis*, for it is the *Śakti-cakra* that is responsible for *laya* (absorption) and *udbhava* (emanation).

§ This does not mean 'This *puryaṣṭaka* one must approach and conquer' as Prof. Leidecker has interpreted it in his translation.

† Kallaṭācārya was the pupil of Vasugupta and wrote a *vṛtti* on the *Spandasūtras*. He flourished in the latter half of the 9th Century A.D.

'स्वतन्त्रश्चितिचक्राणां चक्रवर्ती महेश्वरः ।
संवित्तिदेवताचक्रजुष्टः कोऽपि जयत्यसौ ।।

इति । इतिशब्द उपसंहारे, यत् एतावत् उक्तप्रकरणशरीरं तत् सर्वं 'शिवम्—शिवप्राप्तिहेतुत्वात् शिवात् प्रसृतत्वात् शिवस्वरूपाभिन्नत्वात् च शिवमयमेव इति शिवम् ।।

देहप्राणसुखादिभिः प्रतिकलं संरुध्यमानो जनः
पूर्णानन्दघनामिमां न चिनुते माहेश्वरीं स्वां चितिम् ।
मध्येबोधसुधाब्धि विश्वमभितस्तत्फेनपिण्डोपमं
यः पश्येदुपदेशतस्तु कथितः साक्षात्स एकः शिवः ।।

And it has been lauded by me (in the following verse) :

"He who has become independent ruler[184] (i.e. who is no longer under the control of the senses) of the *citicakra* and the great lord, being served by the group of sense-deities,[185] is only a rare being that excels all."

The word '*iti*' in the *sūtra* connotes conclusion. The word 'Śiva' in the *sūtra* means that whatever is the body of the above text (i.e. whatever has been said in the text) is Śiva, because it is a means to the attainment of Śiva. It is Śiva also, because it has come from Śiva, because it is not different from the true nature of Śiva, and because it is indeed Śiva.

Man bound in all the phases of waking, dream and dreamless sleep by the body, *prāṇa*, pleasure etc. does not recognise his own *citi* (consciousness) which is of the nature of the great power and full of perfect bliss.

But he who, owing to this instruction, beholds in the ocean of the nectar of (spiritual) awareness the universe as a mass of its (i.e. of the ocean of the nectar of awareness) foam on all the sides, is said to be Śiva Himself in sooth.

येषां वृत्तः शांकरः शक्तिपातो
येऽनभ्यासात्तीक्ष्णयुक्तिष्वयोग्याः ।
शक्ता ज्ञातुं नेश्वरप्रत्यभिज्ञा-
मुक्तस्तेषामेष तत्त्वोपदेशः ॥

समाप्तमिदं प्रत्यभिज्ञाहृदयम् ॥

कृतिस्तत्रभवन्महामाहेश्वराचार्यवर्यश्रीमदभिनवगुप्तपादपद्मोपजीविनः श्रीमतो राजानकक्षेमराजाचार्यस्य ॥

शुभमस्तु ॥

This instruction in the truth has been given for those to whom has accrued the descent of Śakti wrought by Śiva, but who for want of the discipline of serious study are unfit for keen arguments, and are hence incapable of understanding the *Īśvara-pratyabhijñā* (i.e. the *Pratyabhijñā* philosophy by Utpaladeva).

Concluded is this *Pratyabhijñāhṛdaya* (The Secret of Recognition).

This work [book] is by the glorious teacher, Rājānaka Kṣemaraja, dependent on the lotus-feet of the glorious Abhinavagupta, the best among the venerable, great Śaiva teachers.

May there be welfare [for all] !

NOTES

1. Recognition—This is the doctrine which teaches that the individual self (*nara* or *jiva*) is identical with the Universal Self (Śiva). He has forgotten his Real Self owing to the limitations of his psycho-physical mechanism. The Śaiva doctrine of Kashmir is called *Pratyabhijñā-darśana* or the Philosophy of Recognition because it brings home to the individual the truth that once he recognises his Real Self, he will be free from his ego-hood which is the product of his identification of himself with his psycho-physical mechanism, and will thus realize that his Real Self is identical with the Universal Self. *Īsvara-pratyabhijñā-vimarśini* by Abhinavagupta gives the following exposition of *Pratyabhijñā*.

"प्रतीपमात्माभिमुख्येन ज्ञानं प्रकाशः प्रत्यभिज्ञा। प्रतीपम् इति—स्वात्मावभासो हि न अननुभूतपूर्वोऽविच्छिन्नप्रकाशत्वात् तस्य, स तु तच्छक्त्यैवविच्छिन्न इव विकल्पित इव लक्ष्यते इति वक्ष्यते। प्रत्यभिज्ञा च–भातभासमानरूपानुसंधानात्मिका, स एवायं चैत्र-इति प्रतिसन्धानेन अभिमुखीभूते वस्तुनि ज्ञानम्; लोकेऽपि एतत्पुत्र एवंगुण एवंरूपक इत्येवं वा, अन्ततोऽपि सामान्यात्मना वा ज्ञातस्य पुनरभिमुखीभावावसरे प्रतिसंधितप्राणितमेव ज्ञानं प्रत्यभिज्ञा—इति व्यवह्रियते। इहापि प्रसिद्धपुराणसिद्धान्तागमानुमानादिविहितपूर्णशक्तिस्वभाव ईश्वरे, सति स्वात्मन्यभिमुखीभूते तत्प्रतिसन्धानेन ज्ञानम् उदेति, नूनं स एव ईश्वरोऽहम्—इति" (p. १९-२०)

"Prati+abhi+jñā = pratyabhijñā, 'Prati' means *pratipam* i.e. contrary, in other words though known, now appearing as forgotten through delusion 'Abhi' means facing i.e. close at hand. 'Jñā' means illumination or knowledge. So Pratyabhijñā means re-cognition of the real self. 'Pratīpam' implies that it is not that the consciousness of self has not been a fact of experience before, for Self is a light that can never be cut off (i.e. it is an ever-present light), but that, as will be explained in the sequel, through its own Power, it appears as though cut off or limited. Recognition (Pratyabhijñā) consists in the unification of what appeared before with what is appearing now, as in the judgement "This is the same Caitra". It is a cognition by recollection, referring to what is directly present.

In ordinary life also, recognition consists in unification of experiences at the time of a subsequent appearance of one who was known before either in general terms, or in particular as 'the son of so and so, of such and such qualities and description', or in a statement like 'so and so has been made to be recognised by the king'.

In the present context also, the knowledge of the Lord as one who has perfect power, having been acquired through the well-known Purāṇas, Siddhānta Āgama, inference etc., and the immediate experience of one's Self being there, *re-cognition* arises, through the unification of the two experiences, in the form "Certainly, I am that very Lord".

This system is also known as Trika darśana i.e. the system of the triad, viz., (1) Nara, the bound Soul (2) Śakti, the divine power and (3) Śiva, the lord who releases the bound soul from his bondage. This is a mystic philosophy, describing all these three conditions.

It is also called *Spandaśāstra* or the system of vibration, because it is to the vibrating energy or Śakti of Śiva that the world-process owes its existence.

2. Śiva—This is derived from the root *śi* (to lie), and from the root *śvi* (to cut asunder). Both these meanings are implied in Śiva. Śiva is one 'in whom all things (viz., all objects and subjects) lie'. He is also one who cuts asunder (*śyati pāpam iti Śivaḥ*) all sins. Śiva is thus both the fundamental ground of all reality and the supreme Benevolence or Good who by His grace saves all. He is the supreme or Absolute both from the metaphysical and soteriological point of view. The name Śiva for the Highest Reality is, therefore, a very happy choice. Śiva is the Highest Reality as well as the Highest Good.

In addition to Pratyabhijñā, Trika, and Spanda, this system is also known as Śaiva-darśana or Bhairava-darśana i.e., the system positing Śiva as the all-of-reality-and good. As this system is non-dual, it is sometimes called Kashmirian Śaiva philosophy in order to distinguish it from the Śaiva philosophy of the South which is dual.

3. *Satatam*—eternally, may be read with *namaḥ* or with *pañcakṛtya-vidhāyine*. In the former case, it would mean 'my eternal adoration to Śiva'. In the latter case it would mean 'my adoration to Śiva who eternally brings about the five processes'. The latter construction is better as it indicates that Śiva's activity is incessant.

4. *Pañcakṛtya* or the five acts brought about by Śiva are :—

(1) *Sṛṣṭi*—Letting go; casting out of oneself. The usual translation 'creation' is misleading. Creation implies that the creator acts upon an external material, and thus brings about the world-process. This translation does not do justice to the Indian point of view, particularly to the point of view of Śaiva philosophy. Sṛṣṭi is derived from the root *sṛj* which means 'to let go', to pour forth', 'to project. This implies that the world-process is already implicitly contained in Śiva. He only lets it go or projects it out of himself. He has not to work on an external material in order to bring about the world-process. According to Śaiva philosophy, the world is not a creation, but an emanation; it is a theophany.

(2) *Sthiti*—maintenance (of the world-process).

(3) *Saṁhāra* or *Saṁhṛti*—withdrawal or re-absorption. It does not mean destruction. There is no destruction of the world. It is only re-absorbed by Śiva for a time. Destruction is only a metaphorical and secondary sense of *saṁhāra*, not its primary sense.

(4) *Vilaya* or *pidhāna*—concealment of the real nature of the Self.

(5) *Anugraha*—grace.

These five *kṛtyas* imply that Śiva lets go the universe out of himself, imparts existence to it and finally withdraws it into himself only to let it appear again. This makes a cycle which is called a *kalpa*. There is no final end to the world-process. The cosmic process is repeated from eternity to eternity.

Anugraha is the act of grace by which Śiva brings about the liberation of man. The first four *kṛtyas* are cosmological, the last is soteriological. The five *kṛtyas* are not an artificial mixture of two standpoints—one cosmological and the other soteriological. Rather *anugraha* is the *raison d'etre* of the first four *kṛtyas*, it is that for the sake of which the first four *kṛtyas*, come into play. It expresses the abounding love of Śiva.

5. *Paramārtha—Parama+artha*: *Parama* means the Highest; *artha* means both 'reality' and 'goal or value'. *Paramārtha* connotes both the Highest Reality and the Highest value. According to Indian thought, the Highest Reality is also the Highest Value of man. In the realization of the Highest Reality consists the meaning and purpose of human life.

6. *Svātma* may mean either one's nature or one's self. In the former case, the line '*cidānandaghana-svātma-paramārthāva-bhāsane*' would mean 'who makes manifest the Highest Reality (which is at the same time the Highest Value) whose *nature* is *cidānandaghana* i.e.,.a mass of consciousness and bliss or compact consciousness and bliss. In the latter case, it would mean 'who makes manifest the Highest Reality (which is at the same time the Highest Value), viz., His Self (which is also the Real Self of each individual) that is a mass of consciousness and bliss'. There is a *double entendre* in *svātma* viz., His Self (the self of Śiva) and the self of each individual, the implication being that His Self is identical with the Real Self of each. This translation is preferable, as it is more in line with the general tenor of this system.

7. Cidānandaghana—mass of consciousness and bliss. In Śāṅkara Vedānta, the expression used is generally 'saccid-ānanda. i.e., *sat* (existence) *cit* (consciousness) and *ānanda* (bliss). In this system, *sat* has been dropped as superfluous, for according to it, *cit* or consciousness alone is *sat* or real. *Cit* and *sat* — consciousness and existence or reality are synonymous. There can be nothing outside consciousness which may be called existent or real. Śaṅkara also says, "*Sat eva bodha, bodha eva sattā*" i.e., Existence itself is consciousness, and consciousness itself is existence.

8. *Upaniṣat—upa-ni-sad* (sit) i.e. sitting down near to or sitting down at the feet of another (i.e., the teacher) to listen to his words. It, therefore, has come to mean *rahasya* or secret knowledge obtained in this manner. It is equivalent to secret or esoteric doctrine. The word has also been interpreted by Śaṅkara as 'destruction (of ignorance) by revealing the know-

ledge of the supreme spirit'. Here the word has been used in the sense of 'secret or esoteric doctrine'.

9. Śaṁkara—*Śaṁ karoti iti Śaṁkaraḥ*, one who brings about happiness and welfare is Śaṁkara. This is another name of Śiva. *Śāṁkaropaniṣat*, therefore, means the esoteric doctrine pertaining to Śaṁkara or Śiva i.e,, the esoteric system known as Śaiva philosophy.

10. *Saṁsāra—Saṁsarati iti saṁsāraḥ* i.e., 'that which is always on the move'; that which is continuous 'pro-cess'. The word 'world, or universe' can hardly do justice to this idea. Etymologically the word '*saṁsāra*' also means 'wandering through' (a succession of states) of the *jīva* or the individual soul. It is in this sense that *saṁsāra* is called *viṣa* or poison here. It is not the world *qua* world which is poison, but the 'wandering through' of the *jiva* as a being disintegrated from Reality, cut off from his Innermost Centre, which is poison. *Viṣa* is derived from the root *viṣ* of the third conjugation (*veveṣṭi*), meaning 'to pervade', hence anything actively pernicious i.e., poison. The root '*viṣ*' in the fourth conjugation (*viṣṇāti*) means also 'to separate, to disjoin'. There may be a suggestion here that *saṁsāra* is *viṣa* because it disjoins us, disintegrates us from Śiva—(the Highest Reality).

11. *Samāveśa*—This is the noun form of *sam-ā-viś*, meaning to enter into. *Samāveśa*, therefore, means mergence or identification. *Samāveśa* with the Highest Lord means identification of the individual self with the Universal Self. The individual, in this state, feels that he is nothing else than Śiva. *Samāveśa*, also means taking possession of the individual by the Divine. The outcome is the same, viz., identification with Śiva. According to Abhinavagupta, *āveśa* means the subordination or disappearance of the personal nature of the aspirant and his identification with the divine nature of Śiva.

"Āveśaśca asvatantrasya svatadrūpanimajjanāt. Paratadrūpatā Śambhorādyācchaktyavibhāginaḥ" *Tantrāloka*—I volume I Āhnika, v. 173.

12. *Śakti* is the energy of *Śiva*, and therefore, not different from him. With this, he brings about *pañcakṛtya* or the five cosmic processes. Śakti-*pāta* means the descent of *Śākti*. *Śākti*-

pāta on an individual means the imparting of *anugraha* or grace to him.

13. *Sūtra*—Lit., 'thread'; hence, it has come to mean that which like a thread runs through or holds together certain ideas; a rule; a formula; a direction. Cp. Latin, *sutura*, English, *suture*.

A *Sūtra* must contain the fewest possible words, must be free from ambiguity, must be meaningful and comprehensive, must not contain useless words and pauses and must be faultless.

14. *Svatantrā*—this is an adjective qualifying *Citi*. This means dependent only on itself and nothing else. It means that it is absolved of all conditions, and is free to do anything it likes. The word Svatantra, has therefore, been rendered by two words; viz., absolute, and of its own free-will.

15. *Citi*—This means universal consciousness-power and is feminine gender in Sanskrit. '*Cit*' is generally used for Śiva and '*citi*' for His Śakti. They are distinguished from *citta* which means 'individual consciousness'.

16. *Siddhi*—means effectuation which includes (1) *prakāśana* or *sṛṣṭi*—emanation (2) *sthiti*—maintenance of what is emanated, and (3) *saṁhāra*, withdrawal or re-absorption.

17. *Sadāśivādeḥ bhūmyantasya*—from Sadāśiva down to the earth. According to this system, there are 36 *tattvas* or principles. These are divisible into two; viz., the *Śuddha adhvā*, the pure or the supramundane way or course and the *aśuddha adhvā* or the impure i.e. the mundane way or course. *Śuddha adhvā* is that which is above *Māyā* in which there is no difference between the knower and the known. *Aśuddha adhvā* is that where difference begins right up to the earth. The 36 *tattvas* are given below in a descending order from Śiva, the Supreme principle.

Above manifestation

1. *Śiva*, the Highest Principle or universal consciousness. In this, *cit* or consciousness is predominant.
2. *Śakti* Śiva's inseparable conscious energy. In this *ānanda* or bliss is predominant.

   These two *tattvas* are the source of all manifestation.

Śudha adhvā Supramundane manifestation

3. *Sadāśiva* i.e, the ever benevolent. In this *tattva ahantā* or I-consciousness and *icchā* or Will are predominant. Idaṁtā or this-consciousness (i.e. world-consciousness) is not so prominent. It is also called *sādākhya* tattva, for it is the state in which there is the first notion of 'being' (*sat ākhyā yataḥ*). It is the incipient world-experience. The world is in an indistinct state at this stage. The consciousness of this state is *Aham idam*—'I am this'. There is no distinction between I and 'this' (the universe). This is a state of perfect identity.
4. *Īśvara,* i.e. the Lord. In this both I-consciousness and world-consciousness are equally prominent, and *jñāna* or knowledge is predominant. The consciousness of this state is '*Idam aham*'—'This is I'—the universe is I. The universe has come distinctly into consciousness but still as identical with the Divine Self. This is a state of *abheda* i.e. non-difference between the 'I' or Self and 'this' or the universe.
5. *Vidyā* or *Śuddhavidyā* or *Sadvidyā* pure, unlimited knowledge. In this there is the consciousness—*Aham idam ca*—'I am I and also this (universe)'. This state is one of *bhedābheda* i.e. the universe is a distinct object to consciousness, yet its distinction is overcome in Self-consciousness. It appears only as an aspect of the Self. This is a state of 'identity in difference'. *Kriyā* or action is predominant here. The first five—from *Śiva* to *Sadvidyā*—are called *Śuddha adhvā,* because the relationship of subject and object is a single unit upto this stage i.e. the object is perceived as a part of the subject; there is no veiling of the Self so far. These five *tattvas* represent the universal aspect of consciousness.

Aśuddha adhvā or mundane manifestation

6. Māyā, the universally formative or limiting principle. Sometimes, this is not included in the *Kañcukas*, as it is a principle superior to the *Kañcukas* and gives rise to the *Kañcukas*. This veils the real Self and brings about the consciousness of difference and plurality.

The Five Kañcukas (coverings) of Māyā

7. *Kalā*, i.e. limitation in respect of authorship or efficacy.
8. *Vidyā*, knowledge i.e. limitation in respect of knowledge.
9. *Rāga*, inclination, limitation of fulness, giving rise to desires for various objects, e.g., I may enjoy this, I may own that etc.
10. *Kāla* i.e. limitation of eternity giving rise to division of past, present, and future.
11. *Niyati*—Restriction i.e. limitation of freedom, giving rise to limitation of space and cause.
12. *Puruṣa*—when the Divine by his Māyā veils His real Self and accepts the status of a limited experient, he is known as *Puruṣa*. At this stage the *Sarvakartṛtva* or omnipotence of the Divine is reduced to *kalā* or limited authorship, His *sarvajñatva* or omniscience is reduced to *vidyā* or limited knowledge; His *pūrṇatva* or all-fulfilment is reduced to *rāga* or want and desire; His *nityatva* or eternity is reduced to *kāla* or time-division; His *vyāpakatva* or omnipresence or all-pervasiveness is reduced to *niyati* or limitation in space or His *svātantrya* is reduced to cause-effect relationship.

    The principles from *Kalā* to *Niyati* are generally known as the five *kañcukas* or coverings, veils of Māyā put on by the Divine.

13. *Prakṛti*—the root or matrix of objectivity from Buddhi down to earth.
14. *Buddhi*, the ascertaining intelligence.
15. *Ahaṁkāra*, the ego-making principle.
16. *Manas*, the conceptive consciousness.

17-21. The five *jñānendriyas* or organs of perception (audition, touch, vision, taste, and smell).

22-26—The five organs of action (*karmendriyas*)

27-31—The five *tanmātras* i.e. the undifferentiated origins of the five perceptions.

32-36—The five *mahābhūtas*; the gross-elements, viz., *ākāśa* (ether), *vāyu* (air), *agni* (fire), *āpas* (water) and *bhūmi* (earth).

18. *Parapramātṛ* means the Highest Experient. *Pramātṛ* means measurer or the subject of experience. The highest experient is *parama-Śiva*, the highest Śiva.

19. *Parāśakti*—the highest Śakti. This is distinguished from the subsidiary *śaktis* that pervade the universe and bring about all kinds of things. They are various aspects of the highest *Śakti*. Śakti means divine consciousness or conscious energy which is non-distinct from Śiva. It is Śiva himself in his active aspect of manifestation and grace.

20. *Vimarśa*—*Vi*+*mṛś*. The root *mṛś* means to touch. *Vimṛś* means to touch mentally. It is a highly technical term of this system. Paramaśiva, the ultimate reality is not only *prakāśa* or luminous consciousness, but also *Vimarśa* i.e. conscious of its consciousness. *Vimarśa* is Self-consciousness or pure I-consciousness of the highest Reality. It is this *Vimarśa* or self-consciousness of reality that brings about the emergence of the universe (*sṛṣṭi*), its manifestation (*sthiti*) and its withdrawal (*saṁhāra*) into it again as identical with its joy of pure I-consciousness. *Vimarśa* assumes three moments, viz., going out of itself (*sṛṣṭi*), maintaining its continued existence (*sthiti*) and then returning to itself (*saṁhāra*).

> cf. "Iha khalu parameśvaraḥ prakāśātmā; prakāśaśca vimarśa-svabhāvaḥ; vimarśo nāma viśvākāreṇa, viśvaprakāśanena, viśvasaṁharaṇena ca akṛtrimāham iti visphuraṇam".—*Parāprāveśika*, pp. 1-2, Kashmir Sanskrit Series.

The entire universe is already contained in the highest consciousness or the highest Self even as the variegated plumage of the peacock is already contained in the plasma of its egg (*mayūrāṇḍarasa-nyāyena*). *Vimarśa* is the positing of this Self which leads to manifestation.

21. *Śiva-bhaṭṭāraka*—The word *bhaṭṭāraka* is the same as *bhaṭṭāra* which again is the same as the word *bhaṭṭa*. The word is derived from the root *bhaṭ* of the first conjugation which means to 'nourish'. The word *bhaṭṭa* or *bhaṭṭāra* or *bhaṭṭāraka* literally means 'the lord that nourishes or supports'. The word *bhaṭṭāra* or *bhaṭṭāraka* means venerable lord. This has been attached to Śiva to show reverence.

22. *Nityodita*—*Nitya*+*udita*. *Udita* is formed from ud+$\sqrt{\text{i}}$+kta—that which is gone up, risen. *Nityodita* is eternally risen. In this system it is generally not the word *nitya* (eternal) that is used for the foundational consciousness, but *nityodita* i.e.

ever-risen, ever-existent. *Nityodita* is that which never sets, but is always risen. The foundational consciousness never takes a holiday. Whatever both rises and sets is called *śāntodita*', but that which never sets, but is always risen is called '*nityodita*'. It is also called *nityodita* because the system wants to emphasize the fact that the eternal consciousness is ever active; there is always *spanda* or vibration in it.

23. *Pramātṛ* (lit. measurer), subject of knowledge.

24. *Pramāṇa* (lit. instrument of knowledge) means of knowledge, proof of knowledge.

25. *Prameya* (lit. to be measured, measurable) the known or object of knowledge.

26. *Baindavī Kalā—paraḥ pramātā. Vetti iti vinduḥ* (*binduḥ*) from the root vid (to know). The highest Self or consciousness which is the knower is known as Bindu. *Bindoriyam iti baindavī. Baindavī* means 'of *bindu*', 'pertaining to *bindu*'. *Kalā* means *śakti. Baindavī kalā* means the power of knowership of the highest Self or consciousness, i.e. the power of Self-consciousness. Here it means that power of the Self by which it is always the subject, never the object. In this verse, feet are compared to *pramāṇa* (means of proof); the head is compared to *pramātā*, the knowing Self. Just as it is impossible for one to catch up the shadow of one's head with one's feet, for the shadow of the head always eludes it, even so is it impossible to know the knower (*pramātā*) by the various means of knowing for the various means owe their own existence to the knower.

27. *Samarasa*—one having the same feeling or consciousness. *Sāmarasya* therefore, means identity of consciousness. In *Saṁhāra* or withdrawal, *Citi* reduces the universe to sameness with the Highest Reality. The Foundational Consciousness is both the alpha and the omega of the universe.

28. *Svatantrā—Citi* or the divine consciousness is called *svatantrā*, because whether it is *sṛṣṭi* (manifestation), *sthiti* (maintenance of the manifestation), *saṁhāra* (withdrawing or reducing the universe to oneness with herself), she is sovereign i.e. does not depend upon any extraneous condition.

29. *Viśva-siddhi* may also mean the effectuation of both *bhoga* (enjoyment of the bliss of real I-consciousness) and *mokṣa*

(liberation). When the absolute free-will of *citi* is recognised she brings about real enjoyment as well as freedom from limitation. In this sense also she is the cause of *viśva-siddhi.*

30. *Pramāṇopārohakrameṇa,* by gradual mounting, beginning with knowledge etc. From the known or *prameya* one has to mount to *pramāṇa* or knowledge; from knowledge one has to mount to the *pramātā* or the knower, to the highest Self. All *pramāṇas* rest in the *pramātā,* the knower.

31. *Brahmavāda* (the doctrine of Brahman) refers to Śaṅkara-vedānta in which Brahman is said to be nonactive.

32. *Darpaṇe nagaravat*—Just as a city appearing in a mirror is nothing different from the mirror, but appears as something different, even so the universe appearing in *citi* is nothing different from it, though it appears as different.

33. *Sadāśiva tattva* may be said to be the first principle of manifestation. Out of the Śiva-śakti state emerges *Sadāśiva tattva* where consciousness is of the form, 'I am this'. 'This' (*idantā*) here refers to the total universe. I (*ahantā*) refers to the Divine Experient. It is the absolute or universal I. The first consciousness of the absolute in manifestation is, 'I am this'. The 'this' (*idantā*) or the entire universe is already implicity contained in the absolute consciousness, but when it begins to posit the I as the 'this, the 'this' becomes the first glimmer of the universe to be. This is, however, a stage of consciousness where the 'this' aspect is in an incipient, germinal form, greatly dominated by the 'I' aspect (*ahantācchādita-asphuṭa-idantāmayam*) where the *viśva* or universe is both different and non-different (*parāpara rūpam*) from Sadāśiva. In this *Icchā* or Will is predominant. In the consciousness, "*I am* this", existence or being is cleary posited; hence this principle is also known as *sādākhya-tattva* (Sat = Being). The system now starts giving a hierarchy of individual experients. Corresponding to the universal experient or Sadāśiva is the individual (mystic) experient, designated *mantramaheśvara* who has realized *Sadāśiva tattva* and whose experience is, therefore, of the form—'I am this'. The whole universe is identified with his Self.

34. *Īśvara tattva* is the next stage of manifestation in which the consciousness of an 'I' and a 'this' is both equally

prominent. The ideal universe which is involved in the absolute consciousness becomes more clearly defined as a 'this' at this stage. *Jñāna* is predominant in this *tattva*. Corresponding to this is the individual (*mystic*) experient known as Mantreśvara who has realized the *Īśvaratattva*, whose consciousness is also of the form 'I am this', in which the universe is no longer an indistinct 'this' but is as clearly defined as the consciousness of 'I', and in which the universe is identical with the Self. The consciousness of Sadāśiva is '*Ahamidam*—'I am this'. The consciousness of Īśvara is '*Idamaham*'—"This am I'.

35. *Vidyā* or *Śuddha Vidyā* is the stage where the consciousness of both 'I' (the experient) and the 'this' (the universe) is distinct, and where diversity or *bheda* begins, though there is unity in diversity at this stage. *Kriyā* is predominant in this *tattva*. Corresponding to this, there are the experients called Mantras who see diversity, though it is diversity-in-unity. The Lord who rules over these experients is called Anantabhaṭṭāraka. The consciousness of this stage is *Idam ca Aham ca* or *Aham idam ca*—the universe as different but also as, belonging to me. At this stage, though the 'this' appears as distinct from 'I', yet it is only an aspect of 'I'. It is *distinct* from 'I', but not *different*. Hence the consciousness of this stage is known as *Śuddha Vidyā*.

36. *Vijñānākala* is the experient of the stage below *Śuddha Vidyā* but above Māyā. Here the experient is devoid of agency; he is pure awareness. His field of experience consists of *sakalas*, and *pralayākalas*. He has a sense of identity with his field of experience (*tadabhedasāram*).

He is free from *Māyīya* and *Kārma mala*, but is still subject to *Āṇava mala*.

37. In this state, the experient has neither the clear consciousness of *aham* (I) nor of *idam* (this). His I-consciousness is identical with a void like the void that one experiences in deep sleep. He has the feeling of a vague something which is practically nothing. The *Palayākala-pramātā* is identified with the *prakṛti* at the time of dissolution. The *yogins* who have an experience only of the void are also like the *pralayākala-pramātā*. He is free from *Kārma mala* but is subject to *Āṇava* and *Māyīyamala*.

38. The *sakalas* are the *devas* (gods) and *jivas* (individual

selves) who have no true knowledge of Self, and whose consciousness is only that of diversity. The average human being belongs to this level. The *Sakalas* are subject to all the three *malas—Āṇava*, *Māyīya* and *Kārma*.

39. The suggestion is that in this state *vimarśa* is latent; only *prakāśa* is predominant.

We may now gather up in a tabular form (see p. 130) the details of the third sūtra.

From Vijñānākala upto Sakala, there is no presiding deity, because the operation of Mahāmāyā begins from the stage of Vijñānākala and also because ignorance begins from the Mahāmāyā stage.

40. *Anāśrita-Śiva-paryāya—anāśrita* i.e. unrelated to anything; lit., whose synonym is Śiva who has no objective content yet. This is a state below Śaktitattva and above Sadāśivatattva. This, however, is only an *avasthā*, a state, not a *tattva*. This refers to that phase of reality where *Śakti* begins temporarily to veil the Self, and thus to isolate the universe from the Self, producing *akhyāti* ignorance of its real nature. This is why *śakti* is said to be '*sva-svarūpāpohanātmākhyātiṁayi niṣedhavyāpārarūpā*' (*Paramārthasāra*, p. 10) i.e. Śakti brings about *akhyāti* by negating or isolating the universe from the Self and thus veiling its real nature. The full experience of Self is that in which I and the This or the Universe are one. The loss of this Experience—Whole is *saṁsāra*; the regaining of this Experience—whole or full Experience of the Self is *mukti*.

41. *Śūnyātiśūnyatayā*—being as yet more void than the void itself. It is called *śūnya* here from the point of view of objective manifestation, from the standpoint of the negation of the universe, i.e. from the point of view of absence of objective content or objectivity.

42. *Triśiromate*—the mystical doctrine concerning the three-headed Bhairava. The three heads of god, Bhairava are a symbolic representation of the three Śaktis of the Divine, viz., Parā, Parāparā, and Aparā. The Parā is the supreme state in which there is no distinction or difference whatsoever between Śiva and Śakti. Parāparā is that state (of manifestation) in which there is identity-in-distinction. Aparā is that state in which there is complete difference.

NOTE 39: Details of Sūtra 3—तन्नाना अनुरूपग्राह्यग्राहकभेदात्

Tattva 1	*The Presiding Deity* 2	*The experient* 3	*Corresponding field of experience* 4
1. Śiva	Śiva	Śiva Pramātā	All existence is mere Prakāśa or Śiva
2. Sadāśiva. In this, Icchā or Will is predominant	Sadāśiva-bhaṭṭāraka	Mantra-maheśvara. The experience of 'I' or Śiva is clear but there is also a dim experience of the Universe.	Indistinct experience of the universe, not yet distinct from Self experience
3. Īśvara tattva In this, jñāna or knowledge is predominant	Īśvara-bhaṭṭāraka	Mantreśvara who like Īśvara has a distinct experience of both 'I' and the Universe but the Universe is only an aspect of Self	Experience of Self and the universe as both distinct and equally matched, but the universe is still an aspect of the Self
4. Śuddhavidyā-tattva or Sadvidyā tattva. In this, Kriyā or action is predominant	Ananta-bhaṭṭāraka	Mantra who has an experience of both 'I' and the universe as separate but the universe as closely related to Self	Experience of difference from everything and yet everything appearing as closely related to the Self
5. Mahāmāyā tattva		Vijñānākala. He has knowledge but is devoid of agency. He is free from Māyīya and Kārma mala but is still subject to *āṇava malas*	All the pralayākalas, and Sakalas.
6. Māyātattva		Pralayākala or Pralayakavelī or Śūnya-pramātā. He is free from Kārma mala but is still subject to Āṇava and Māyīya malas.	Mere void
7. The remaining tattvas upto the earth.		Sakala, from the *devas* upto the plant and minerals. This is subject to all the three malas āṇava, māyīya and Kārma mala.	Experiencing all things as differing from one another and from the Self.

43. *Sarvadevamayaḥ kāyaḥ*—the universe is considered to be like a body constituted by all the gods. The gods here symbolize both the *pramātā* and the *prameya*, all the subjects and objects—the experients and the experienced. Another reading is *Sarva-tattva-mayaḥ kāyaḥ*—the body of the universe is constituted by all the *tattvas*.

44. *Priye*—dear one or my dear. The Āgama literature is generally in the form of a dialogue between Śiva and his consort Pārvati. Hence, 'Priye'—O, dear one.

45. Bhairava means the terrible one who destroys the weakness of the lower self. This is the name of Śiva. Bhairava is constituted of three letters, *bha*, *ra*, and *va*. The hermeneutic interpretation of Bhairava, therefore, is that '*bha*' indicates. '*bharaṇa*'—maintenance of the universe, '*ra*' indicates '*ravaṇa*' —i.e., withdrawal of the universe, '*va*' indicates '*vamana*'—ejecting or letting go of the universe, i.e., manifestation of the universe. Thus, Bhairava indicates all the three aspects of the Divine, viz., *Sṛṣṭi* (manifestation), *sthiti* (maintenance) and *Saṁhāra* (withdrawal). Bhairava has been called 'three-headed', because as stated above in note 42 the three heads are a symbolic representation of the three śaktis of Bhairava, viz., *parā*, *parāparā*, and *aparā* or because the three heads are a symbolic representation of Nara, Śakti, and Śiva.

46. It has not yet been possible to trace the source of this verse. The idea in this verse is expressed in the form of a paradox. But what does 'akhyāti'—nescience or non-knowledge mean ? Does it appear or not ? In other words—is it experienced or not ? If *akhyāti* is never experienced, then it is nothing and only *khyāti* or knowledge remains. If it is said that *akhyāti* does appear (i.e. is experienced), then being *khyāti* or experience, *khyāti* again remains. So *khyāti* or knowledge cannot be eliminated in any case.

47. The reference is to *Spandakārikā*, ch. II, vv. 3-4.

48. *Vikalpa* means difference of perception; an idea as different from other ideas; differentiation. Vikalpanam (Viśeṣeṇa vividhena kalpanam) = ideating a 'this' as different from 'that', differentiation-making activity of the mind. *Vikalpa* is the nature of the individual mind (*citta*) which goes on making differentiation between one thing and another.

Compare the vivṛti of Yogarāja on verse 11 of *Paramārthasāra* of Abhinavagupta, *'Vikalpo hi anyāpoha-lakṣaṇo'dvayam ghaṭāghaṭa-rūpam ākṣipan, aghaṭāt vyavacchinnam ghaṭam niścinoti'* p. 33, i.e., *vikalpa* is of the nature of differentiating one thing from another. For instance dividing an experience into jar and non-jar, it marks out the jar from the non-jar, and thus ascertains it as a jar. In *Yoga-Sūtra* of Patañjali, (Samādhi-Pāda, 9), *Vikalpa* means a mere fancy which has no foundation in reality. That is not the meaning here.

What the objector wants to drive at is this. The nature of the individual mind is differentiation-making, knowing 'this' as different from 'that', whereas Śiva or the Universal Consciousness is free of all *Vikalpas* or differentiating ideas. How then can you call the individual experient as non-different from Śiva, so long as the differentiation-making mind of the individual lasts ?

49. Citta means the individual consciousness.

50. Vijñānākala—See note 36.

51. Vidyāpramātṛtā—the experients of vidyā-tattva i.e. Mantras.

52. Sadāśiva, Īśa, Anāśrita-śiva, see notes 33, 34 and 40.

53. Śiva, Sadāśivā, Īśvara, and Śuddhavidyā are together known as Śuddhādhvā—the pure or higher path. Mantra, Mantreśvara, Mantra-maheśvara etc. are Śuddhādhvā experients. Predominance of *cit* is common to both Vidyāpramātāras and Śuddhādhva-pramātāras, but in the former case it is natural, whereas in the latter, it is acquired through the effort of Samādhi.

54. Śūnyapramātṛ, etc. See note 37. The word ādi i.e. etc. includes *sakalas* also.

55. The meaning of the verse is—what is jñāna in the case of Śiva appears as *sattva* in the case of '*paśu*' or *jiva* (the individual), what is *kriyā* in the case of Śiva (the universal, Absolute Consciousness) appears as *rajas* in the individual, what is *māyā* in the case of Śiva appears as *tamas* in the individual.

56. *Sattva*, *rajas*, and *tamas* are the three *guṇas* which are the chief characteristics of Prakṛti, the root principle of manifestation. This has been elaborately described by Sāṅkhya,

and accepted by practically all systems of Hindu philosophy. Guṇa means strand, a constituent, an aspect of Prakṛti. *Sattva* is the aspect of harmony, goodness, enlightenment, and *sukha* or pleasure. *Rajas* is the aspect of movement, activity, and *duḥkha* or commotion. *Tamas* is the aspect of inertia, and *moha* or dullness, indifference.

57. Vikalpa—See note 48.

58. Māyāpramātā is the experient of the impure path—the sphere of limitation. Māyāpramātā includes *pralayākalas* and *sakalas*. See notes 37 and 38 and the table given on p. 130.

59. *Svātantrya* is the abstract noun of *Svatantra* which means one's own rule, not conditioned by any thing outside oneself such as *māyā*. It is the absolute, spontaneous, free will of the divine consciousness, outside the causal chain, the free, creative act of the Universal consciousness.

60. *Mala* : dust, dirt, impurity, taint; dross. Dross is the best English equivalent. *Mala* is what covers and conceals and limits the pure gold of divine consciousness. It is of three forms, viz., *āṇava mala*, *māyīya mala*, and *kārma mala*. As used in this system, *mala* means those cosmic and individualistic limiting conditions which hamper the free expression of the spirit.

Āṇava mala is the mūla-mala, the primal limiting condition which reduces the universal consciousness to an *aṇu*, a small, limited entity. It is a cosmic limiting condition over which the individual has no control. It is owing to this that the *jiva* (individual soul) considers himself *apūrṇa*, imperfect, a separate entity, cut off from the universal consciousness. The greatness of Śiva in this condition is concealed, and the individual forgets his real nature. The *āṇava mala* is brought about in two ways. Bodha or knowledge loses its *svātantrya* or unimpeded power, and *svātantrya* or *śakti* loses its *bodha* or inherent knowledge.

Māyīyamala is the limiting condition brought about by *māyā*, that gives to the soul its gross and subtle body. It is also cosmic. It is *bhinna-vedya-prathā*—that which brings about the consciousness of difference owing to the differing limiting adjuncts of the bodies.

Kārma-mala. It is the *vāsanās* or impressions of actions done by the *jñānendriyas* and *karmendriyas* under the influence of antaḥkaraṇa. It is the force of these *vāsanās* that carries the *jīva* from one life to another.

It may be noted that Vijñānākala has only *āṇava mala*, Pralayākala has two, viz., *āṇava* and *māyīya mala*, and Sakala has all the three viz, *āṇava*, *māyīya*, *and kārma mala.*

61. Of the nature of *Śūnya* i.e. *Śūnya pramātā* or *pralaya-kevali* whose field of experience is the void.

62. *Puryaṣṭaka*—Literally, the city of eight, refers to the subtle body consisting of the five *tanmātras* (i.e., the fundamental undifferentiated essence of the five gross elements) *manas*, *buddhi* and *ahaṅkāra*. · It is also known as *sūkṣmaśarīra* or *liṅga-śarīra* which is the vehicle of the *saṁskāras*.

63. Vide Note No. 17.

64. *Upādhi* (up+ā+dhā) lit., some thing placed near, which affects or limits a thing without entering into it as its constituent.

65. *Sugata* (lit., one who has fared well) is a title of the Buddha. Therefore his followers are known as *Saugatas*.

66. The Mādhyamikas are the followers of the Madhyamaka (the system of the middle way) school of philosophy. They believe in *śūnya* (lit., void) as the fundamental principle.

67. The *Pāñcarātra* or *Bhāgavata* system is the main philosophy of Vaiṣṇavaism. On the origin of *Pāñcarātra*, see Sir R.G. Bhandarkar's "*Vaiṣṇavaism, Śaivism and Minor Religious systems*". The derivation of the word, *Pāñcarātra* is somewhat obscure. Perhaps it refers to some religious rites lasting for five nights. The followers of *Pāñcarātra* are here called *Pāñcarātras*.

68. The word '*prakṛti*' here does not mean the Prakṛti or root-matter of the Sāṅkhyas. *Parā prakṛti* here means the highest cause. The followers of *Pāñcarātra* system consider Vāsudeva both as the material cause and controlling cause of all manifestation.

69. Leidecker believes that *pariṇāma* here does not mean transformation or change, but the Pāñcarātras considered *jīvas*, etc. to be the *pariṇāma* or transformation of Vāsudeva. Śaṅkara while criticizing the *Pāñcarātra* system in his commentary on Brahmasūtra in Utpattyasambhavādhikaraṇa puts its position quite clearly and correctly.

"Teṣām Vāsudevaḥ *parā prakṛtir*—itare Saṅkarṣaṇādayaḥ *kāryam*."

70. Kṣemarāja seems to have made some confusion here. The Pāñcarātras do not consider "*avyakta*" (non-manifest) as the ultimate source, but Vāsudeva who is higher than "*avyakta*"- Śaṅkara puts their position quite correctly in his commentary on Brahmasūtras, in Utpattyasambhavādhikaraṇa:

"तत्र यत् तावदुच्यते योऽसौ नारायणः परोऽव्यक्तात् प्रसिद्धः परमात्मा सर्वात्मा स आत्मनात्मानमनेकधा व्यूह्यावस्थित इति, तन्न निराक्रियते"

71. "Sāṅkhyas" here means 'the followers of Sāṅkhya".

72. See note 36.

73. The Vaiyākaraṇas were the followers of the Grammar School of Philosophy that considered grammar as means of spiritual liberation Their philosophy has been described under the heading "Pāṇini-darśanam" in *Sarva-darśana-saṁgraha*" by Mādhava. The reference is obviously to Bhartṛhari's *Vākyapadīya* which considers *paśyanti* as Śabdabrahma or Reality as Vibration.

74-75. The philosophy of Vyākaraṇa considers the Absolute or Highest Reality as "Śabda-brahman." Śabda (word) is to them not something unconscious but consciousness itself where thought and word are the same and are not yet distinguished. Brahman is the eternal word from which emanates everything. According to the Trika system, the universe of objects and so also of thoughts and words is always in Parama Śiva potentially. This is the stage of the Parāvāk—the highest word which is yet unmanifest. The next stage is that of Paśyantī which is the divine view of the universe in its undifferentiated form, far beyond human experience. Kṣemarāja means to say that the grammarians go only as far as *paśyantī* which is confined to the stage of Sadāśiva but not upto Parāvāk which alone refers to the stage of Parama Śiva. After the *paśyanti*, there is the *madhyamā*, which marks the next stage of the manifestation of the universe from undifferentiated mass to differentiated particulars. Madhyamā, lit., the middle one is thus a link between Paśyantī, the vision of the undifferentiated universe, and Vaikharī, the stage of differentiated particulars, the stage of empirical thought and speech. It is word in a subtle form in the mind or antaḥkaraṇa. In Vaikharī, the 'word' appears separately from 'thought', and 'object'.

76. The āgamas (here' Śaiva-Āgamas) refer to a group of literature containing the doctrine of the Śaivas. 'Āgama' means tradition, that which is handed down from generation to generation.

77. By Ārhatas (the deserving, dignified) is here meant the Jains. They maintain that the universe consists of 'paramāṇus' (atoms of matter) which are eternal. They are subject to change or development inasmuch as they assume different *guṇas* (qualities). The Āgama quoted means to suggest that Jains consider these *guṇas* as the highest reality they have discovered and are unable to go further than the *guṇas*.

78. *Pāñcarātrikas*—Vide note 67.

79. The followers of "tantra" are known as *tāntrikas*. The word "tantra" has been explained in two ways,

(1) from the root 'tan' to expand—that in which the principles of reality are expanded, are elaborately described is "tantra".

(2) from the root "tantra" to control, to harness—that which teaches how to control and harness the various forces of reality is "tantra".

80. *'Kula'* here means *'Śakti'* (the divine manifesting power). The reference here is obviously to the Śāktas, the worshippers of Śakti.

81. *Trika*—The *Pratybhijñā* philosophy is known as *Trika* inasmuch as it describes Parama Śiva or Highest Reality as maninesting itself in a group of three (*trika*), viz., Śiva, Śakti and Nara. From 'et cetera' in Trika etc. may be understood Tripurā or Mahārtha.

82. *Paraśaktipāta*—The grace of the Highest. *Śaktipāta* or grace is of two kinds, viz. *para* (highest) and *apara* (lower). *Paraśaktipāta* or the highest grace connotes the transmutation of the empirical or limited ego into the Fullest Divine Consciousness. Such grace can be imparted only by the Divine. In *apara Śaktipāta* (lower grace), though the ego realizes his identity with the Divine, he is yet unable to realize that the entire universe is only a manifestation of himself and has thus not yet obtained the Fullest Divine consciousness of Śiva.

Apara Śaktipāta (lower grace) can be imparted by a spiritual director or gods.

83. *Vidyā* is one of the five *Kañcukas*—the impure knowledge (*aśuddha-vidyā*). It is the principle of limitation which does not allow the individual to have a synoptic view of reality.

84. *Turīya*, the fourth state of consciousness. In Saṁskṛta 'catur' means 'four'. When *īyat* suffix is added to 'catur', 'ca' is dropped and 't' of *iyat* suffix is dropped (tur+īya), and thus the word becomes 'turīya' which means 'fourth'. Every man's consciousness is in three states—*jāgrat* (waking), *svapna* (dreaming), *suṣupti* (deep sleep). These states are exclusive. When a man is in the waking consciousness, he has no dream or deep sleep consciousness. When he is dreaming, he has no waking or deep sleep consciousness. When he is in deep sleep, he has no dreaming or waking consciousness. In every man, there is a fourth (*turīya*) state of consciousness also which is the witness of the other three states. Turīya is a relative term. It is in relation to the other three states that it is called *turīya* or fourth. There is no succession in *turīya* as there is in the other three states. It is ever present as the witnessing consciousness of the three states. The ego limited by body, prāṇa and *manas* has no experience of *turīya*, although it is always present in him as the background of all the three states. When *avidyā* (the primal ignorance) is removed,—then only man has the experience of *turīya* consciousness. That is the essence of our consciousness which is experienced when the present limitations are transcended. Micro-cosmically, it is the fourth state of consciousness holding together the waking (*jāgrat*), dreaming (*svapna*) and dreamless sleep (*suṣupti*). Macro-cosmically, it is the fourth state holding together the three *kṛtyas*, of *sṛṣṭi*, *sthiti*, and *saṁhāra*. "*Sṛṣṭi-sthiti-saṁhāra-melana-rūpā iyam turīyā*". Just as a string holds together various flowers in a garland, even so it holds together the other three forms of experience and runs through them all. It is *integral awareness*. But it is other than the three states of waking, dream and sleep. Hence it is called the fourth. When an individual consciously experiences *turīyā* state, the sense of difference disappears.

Turīyā has been described as *pūrṇā* (full) from the point of view of *saṁhāra* or withdrawal because in that condition she has withdrawn all that had emanated from her, *kṛśā* or emaciated from the point of view of *udvamana* or emanation because in that condition she is letting go the entities that she had held in her. So Turīyā may be said to be *ubhaya-rūpā* i.e., both full and emaciated. In the highest sense, however, she is *anubhayātmā*, beyond the conditions of fulness and emaciation.

85. For *aṇu* and *mala*, see note 60.

86. Kalā here means limitation in respect of authorship and efficacy. Regarding kalā and other kañcukas, see note 17.

87. *Māyīya-mala*—See note 60.

88. *Kārma-mala*—See note 60.

89. *Kalā.....niyati*—See note 17.

The whole idea of the limitation of the powers of Śiva may be expressed in a tabular form :

Śkati as existing in Śiva	Śakti as existing in the limitation of man
1. Sarvakartṛtva—omnipotence	Kalā—limited authorship or efficacy.
2. Sarvajñatva—omniscience	Vidyā—limitation in respect of knowledge.
3. Pūrṇatva or Nitya-tṛpti—perfection or fullness	Rāga—limitation in respect of desire, i.e., desiring this or that particular.
4. Nityatva—eternity	Kāla—limitation in respect of time.
5. Vyāpakatva or Svātantrya—all pervasiveness or freedom	Niyati—limitation in respect of space and cause.

90. "Īśvarādvaya-darśana" means the system of philosophy which *does not believe in any other principle* (*advaya*) than Īśvara, the Lord. This is the characterization of the Śaiva philosophy of Kashmir which maintains that Śiva is the whole and sole reality. There is 'no second' (*advaya*), i.e., no other principle than Śiva. Īśvara here is a synonym of Śiva. He appears both as the world or the field of experience and the

experient, as the knower (*pramātā*), of knowledge (*pramāṇa*) and the knowable (*prameya*).

91. 'Brahmavādins' refers to those Vedantists who believe that a principle, called Māyā, other than Brahman is responsible for *sṛṣṭi*, *sthiti* and *saṁhāra*. Literally, it means advocates of the Brahman doctrine.

92. *Pañca-vidha-kṛtya*--the five-fold act. For details see note 4. In Sūtra 10, the five-fold act is described from the epistemological point of view.

93. *Śuddhetara-adhvā*=(lit.), (course other than the intrinsic) i.e., the *aśuddhādhvā*, the non-intrinsic course, the extrinsic manifestation: *Śuddhādhvā* is the intrinsic or supramundane manifestation; *aśuddhādhvā* is the mundane or extrinsic manifestation. Sadāśiva, Īśvara, and Śuddhavidyā are in the region of *Śuddha-adhvā* or supramundane manifestation. The *tattvas* from *māyā* to the five gross elements are in the region of *aśuddha-adhvā*, the extrinsic course or mundane manifestation. This has been called *aśuddha-addhvā* or impure course, because in this there is a sense of *bheda* or difference. In *Śudha-addhvā* or the pure course, there is a sense of *abheda* or non-difference.

94. This is called 'vilaya', because the real nature of self is veiled in this state.

95. In the matter of knowledge, the object known in a way becomes one with the knowing subject. The actual *pramiti* (knowledge), divested of the accidents, of the *prameya* (the known object), will be found to be one with the *parmātṛ* (the knowing subject).

96. Here the five-fold act is described particularly from the point of view of the esoteric experience of the yogin. From this point of view, *ābhāsana* is *sṛṣṭi*, *rakti* is *sthiti*, *Vimarśana* is *Saṁhāra*, *bījāvasthāpana* is *vilaya*, and *vilāpana* is *anugraha*. For the meaning of *ābhāsana* etc., see the Commentary.

97. 'Mahārtha' is the esoteric aspect of this system.

98. *Vimarśana* or *camatkāra* is the experience of 'Ah! How wonderful!' It is like the delight of an artistic experience; hence it is called *camatkāra* which means an intuitive flash of artistic experience.

99. The knowledge of the object is called *saṁhāra* here,

because the object is withdrawn. The object as an object disappears and only its knowledge remains.

100. *Haṭhapāka* : There are two ways by means of which an object of experience is brought to sameness with the real essence of the experient, viz., (1) *śānti-praśama* and (2) *haṭhapāka praśama*. Praśama means 'reducing completely the world of experience to oneness with the experient'. The first one is a slow, gradual process: the second, i.e., *haṭhapāka* is a dogged, persistent process. It is not gradual.

101. *Alaṁgrāsa* : *alam+grāsa* : *alam* means *paripūrṇarūpatayā*, *nis-saṁskāratayā*, i.e., fully perfectly, when no impression or germ of *saṁsāra* as separate from consciousness is allowed to remain; *grāsa* is *grasanam* (lit., swallowing)—here it means *svātmasātkaraṇam*—bringing it to sameness with the Self.

102. *Mantras* : 'Mantra' is composed of two letters '*man*' and '*tra*'. '*Man*', implies *mananāt* (by pondering), and '*tra*' implies *trāyate* (protects, saves). *Mantra*, therefore, means that which protects or saves by pondering. *Mantra* is a sacred word or words which, when properly uttered and meditated upon, become efficacious (in all sorts of ways; here in bringing about liberation).

103. Parāvāk—It is *citi* (consciousness-power) which consists of an inner sound born of *non-māyīya* letters. It is ever sounded, ever throbbing. It is the *Svātantrya Śakti*, the free, unfettered, absolute Will-power, the main glorious supreme sovereignty of the Divine, "पूर्णत्वात् परा, वक्ति विश्वमभिलपति प्रत्यवमर्शेन इति च वाक्". It is called *parā*', because it is supreme, perfect. It is called 'vāk', because it sounds forth, utters forth, the universe by its 'I-cosciousness'. Also see notes 74-75.

(Īśvara pr. vi. p. 253).

104. '*a*' to '*kṣa*'. These include all the letters of the Devanāgarī script. These letters according to the Śaiva philosophy represent various *śaktis*.

105. See notes 74-75.

106. See note 48. The *vikalpa*-activity refers to the *vikṣepa* aspect of *Śakti* which projects all kinds of differences. The *ācchādana* or veiling refers to the *āvaraṇa* aspect of *śakti* which throws a veil over the real nature of the Self, and thus

conceals the *avikalpa* stage of the Self. In this one sentence, the writer has referred to both the *vikṣepa* and the *āvaraṇa* aspects of *Śakti*.

107. *Avikalpa* is the distinction-less consciousness. It is the opposite of *vikalpa*. It is mere awareness without a 'this', or 'that'. It is *turyātita avasthā*, a stage of consciousness beyond the *turya*.

108. Brāhmī, lit., means pertaining to Brahmā. The other *śaktis* are, Māheśvari, Kaumārī, Vaiṣṇavī, Vārāhī, Indrāṇī, Cāmuṇḍā and Mahālakṣmī. There are eight classes of letters. The presiding deity of each is as follows :

	Deity	*Class of letter*
1.	Brāhmī	Ka class
2.	Māheśvarī	Ca "
3.	Kaumārī	Ṭa "
4.	Vaiṣṇavī	Ta "
5.	Vārāhī	Pa "
6.	Indrāṇī	Ya "
7.	Cāmuṇḍā	Śa "
8.	Mahālakṣmī	A "

109. The idea is that so long as the soul is in the *paśu* (bound) stage, the *Śakti-cakras* (the *śaktis* with their differentiation making hosts) cause to appear the *sṛṣṭi* and *sthiti*—the emanation and maintenance of *bheda* or difference only, and *saṁhāra* or complete disappearance of *abheda* or non-difference or one-ness. At this stage, consciousness of difference is created and maintained, and consciousness of oneness is completely withdrawn. At the *pati* stage, when bondage of the soul dissolves, the reverse of the previous condition happens. Here the *śaktis* bring about *sṛṣṭi* and *sthiti*, emanation and maintenance of *abheda*, non-difference or one-ness of all, and *saṁhāra* or complete withdrawal of *bheda* or difference Pati stage is of two kinds—(1) *anādisiddha* eternally present as in the case of Śiva and (2) *Yogi-daśā*—that which appears at the stage of *yogin*. It is the latter which is meant by *pati-daśā* here. Prof. Leidecker has given a very fantastic interpretation of this. See note 173, pp. 138-39

of his translation. The text has been completely misunderstood by him here.

It should be borne in mind that at the *pati* stage, the *cakras* (the differentiation-making hosts) of the *śaktis* dissolve, and the *śaktis* begin to function in their pure state. In the *paśu* stage, these are called *khecarī cakra*, *gocarī cakra*, *dikcarī cakra* and *bhūcarī cakra*, but in the *pati* stage, these are called simply *cidgaganacarī or khecarī*, *gocarī*, *dikcarī* and *bhūcarī* respectively.

110. *Bhairava-mudrā*—This has been defined thus :

अन्तर्लक्ष्यो बहिर्दृष्टिर्निमेषोन्मेषवर्जितः ।
इयं सा भैरवीमुद्रा सर्वतन्त्रेषु गोपिता ॥

This is a kind of psycho-physical condition brought about by the following practice :

"Attention should be turned inwards; the gaze should be turned outwards, without the twinkling of the eyes. This is the *mudrā* pertaining to Bhairava, kept secret in all the Tantras."

111. *Śuddha* (*pure*) *vikalpa*—This is the *vikalpa* in which the Sādhaka feels—*Sarvo mamāyam vibhavaḥ*—all this glory of manifestation is of (my) Self, in which he identifies himself with Śiva. It is a total consciousness and the means for passing into *nirvikalpa* or consciousness free from differentiations. This is called *śuddha vikalpa* or pure vikalpa, because though it is still *vikalpa* or mental formulation, it is *śuddha* or pure inasmuch as it is a *mental* formulation of the identity of oneself with the Divine.

112. *Maheśatā*—This is an abstract noun of '*Maheśa*' which means the great Lord (Śiva). Maheśatā or Māheśvarya, therefore, means the power or status of the great Lord, Śiva. It connotes the state in which the soul is perfected and identified with Maheśa, the great Lord or Śiva.

113. *Vikalpas*—See note 48.

114. *Vāmeśvarī*—The author here gives the reason as to why this *śakti* is known as *vāmeśvarī*. The word *vāma* is connected with the verb '*vam*' which means 'to spit out, emit, eject'. The Śakti is called Vāmeśvarī, because she emits or sends forth the universe, out of the Absolute. The word *vāma* also means

'left, reverse, contrary, opposite'. This *śakti* is called Vāmeśvarī also because while in the Śiva state there is unity-consciousness, in the state of Saṁsāra, the *contrary* or *opposite* condition happens, viz., there is difference-consciousness, and also because every one considers the body, prāṇa, etc., to be his Self. This play on the word *vāma* cannot be retained in the translation.

115. *Khecari*, *gocari*, *dikcari* and *bhūcari* are only subspecies of Vāmeśvarī śakti. Khecarī is connected with the *pramātā*, the empirical subject, the limited experient; *gocari* is connected with his *antaḥkaraṇa*, the inner psychic apparatus; *dikcari* is connected with the *bahiṣkaraṇa*, the outer senses; *bhūcari* is connected with the *bhāvas*, existents or outer objects. These *śakti-cakras* indicate the processes of the objectification of the universal consciousness. By *khecarī cakra*, one is reduced from the position of an all-knowing consciousness to that of limited experient; by *gocarī cakra*, he becomes endowed with an inner psychic apparatus, by *dikcarī cakra*, he is endowed with outer senses; by *bhūcari cakra*, he becomes confined to *bhāvas* or external objects.

Khecarī is one that moves in *kha* or *ākāśa*. *Kha* or *ākāśa* is, here, a symbol of consciousness. The *śakti* is called *khecarī*, because her sphere is *kha* or consciousness. *Gocarī* is so called, because her sphere is the inner psychic apparatus. The *saṁskṛta* word '*go*' indicates movement, and thus light-rays, cow, senses are known as '*go*', because they are connected with movement. The *antaḥkaraṇa* is the seat of the senses and sets them in motion; it is the dynamic apparatus of the spirit *par excellence*. Hence it is said to be the sphere of *gocarī*. *Dikcarī* is literally the *śakti* that moves in *dik* or space. The outer senses have to do with the consciousness of space. Hence the outer senses are said to be the sphere of *dikcarī*. The word *bhū* in *bhūcarī* means 'existence' (world). Hence existent objects are the sphere of *bhūcari śakti*. The empirical individual experient, his psychophysical powers, and his objects of experience have all been described here as expressions of various *śakti-cakras*.

116. There are three aspects of *antaḥkaraṇa*, viz., *buddhi*, *ahaṁkāra* and *manas*. Buddhi ascertains; *ahaṁkāra* brings about identification of the Self with the body etc., and assimilation of

experience with oneself, and *manas* determines a thing as this or that.

117. *aiśvaryaśakti* is the sovereign power of the Lord. This is also His *Svātantrya-śakti*, his absolute free Will.

118 and 119. Flashing forth or *sphurattā* is here another name of *prakāśa*. Doership or *kartṛtā* is another name of *vimarśa*. Regarding the distinction between *prakāśa* and *vimarśa*, see note 20.

120. *prāṇa, apāna, samāna śaktis.*

There are five *prāṇas—prāṇa, apāna, samāna, udāna, vyāna*. These are, however, *vāyus* or vital airs. Prāṇas are the *vāyus* that carry out the functions of vegetative life. They are distinct from the body. Like vitalism, Indian philosophy maintains that life is something different from mere matter. Life is maintained by various *prāṇas*. Breath is the most palpable and concrete expression of *prāṇa*. Prāṇa is a comprehensive word covering all the functions of vegetative life. It is, however, divided into various divisions according to various functions. Roughly, *prāṇa* is the vital *vāyu* that goes out, *apāna* is the vital *vāyu* that goes in downwards towards the anus. *Samāna* is the vital *vāyu* that is said to be located in the interior of the body. It helps in *assimilation* of food, etc. Hence it is known as *samāna*. *Vyāna* means going in all directions. It is everywhere in the body. 'Udāna' means 'going upward'. Here the word *śakti* has been used, not *vāyu*. The various *vāyus* are the functions of the various *śaktis* of the same name. By means of *prāṇa*, *apāna* and *samāna śaktis*, one becomes a bound soul (*paśu*); by means of *udāna* and *vyāna śaktis*. one is freed, becomes *pati*.

121. *Kalās* means organs or phases, here those phases which bind the soul to the world.

122. *Puryaṣṭaka*. This is a synonym of the *sūkṣmaśarīra*, the vehicle of the *saṁskāras* which is not cast off at death like the *sthūla śārīra* or the physical body. '*Puri*' means a city and *aṣṭakam* means a group of eight—*puryaṣṭaka* meaning the city of the group of eight. This group of eight consists of the *five tanmātras, manas, buddhi*, and *ahaṁkāra*.

123. *Udāna śakti*. It is the *śakti* which appears when *prāṇa* and *apāna* become equally balanced. Udāna then becomes

active, moves up through the *madhya-dhāma* or *suṣumnā* and brings about the *turya* or fourth state of consciousness.

124. *madhya-dhāma* is the middle *nāḍi* or *suṣumnā*. There are two *nāḍis* running in a parallel way on to the *suṣumnā*. They are not physical but *prāṇic*, and are known as *iḍā* and *piṅgalā*. Prāṇa flows through the *iḍā* and *apāna* flows through the *piṅgalā*. *Suṣumnā* is a *prāṇic nāḍi* running up inside the spinal column towards the brain. Normally the *prāṇa* and *apāna* śaktis alone are active. When, however, through the practice of yoga, *prāṇa* and *apāna* currents are equilibrated the *suṣumnā nāḍi* becomes open, and the *udāna* current flows through it and brings about the *turya* state of consciousness.

125. *Turya* literally means the fourth. The word *catur* means four. The word *turya* is formed by *catur+yat* in which *ca* is dropped and only *tur* remains and *t* of the suffix *yat* is dropped. So we have *tur+ya=turya* meaning the fourth. Normally man's consciousness functions only in three states, viz., waking (*jāgrat*), dreaming (*svapna*), and dreamless sleep (*suṣupti*). When *udāna śakti* becomes active in the *madhya-dhāma* or *suṣumnā*, one develops the consciousness of *turya* or the fourth state in which one has unity-consciousness and the sense of difference disappears. This consciousness is full of bliss.

In the first or waking condition, the body, *prāṇa*, *manas* and senses are active. In the second or dreaming condition, the *prāṇa* and *manas* alone are active. In the third or the state of deep sleep, even the *manas* stops functioning, and *ātman* or pure consciousness is in association with mere void. In the *turya* or fourth state, *ātman* is detached from these limitations, and remains pure consciousness and bliss (*cidānandaghana*). Our waking, dream and deep sleep states, are detached from each other i.e. during waking state we do not have the dream and deep sleep consciousness; during dream state, we do not have the waking and deep sleep consciousness; during deep sleep state, we do not have the waking and dream consciousness. When we are in one state, we are not aware of the other two states, but *turya* is *integral awareness* i.e. it is always aware or conscious of all the three states; it is not cut off from any of the states. When *turya* awareness is established, the habit of *manas*, viz., of knowing things in parts or snippets, of departmentalisation in awareness is reduced. Turya is a consciousness which is aware of all the three states: waking, dream and deep sleep. It is not under the influence of *māyā* which brings about a sense of difference. *Turya* or fourth is a relative word. It is called *turya* or *turīya* (fourth) with reference to the three states of waking, dreem and deep sleep. The three states of waking, dream and deep sleep do not disappear, only the *turya* or the fourth awareness is always aware of all the three states; it is not cut off from any of the three states. Though running through all the three states, the *turya* is unaffected by them, for it is completely free from any impression of subject-object duality, being pure consciousness and bliss; hence while running through them all, it transcends them all. Cf. Yogarāja's commentary on verse 35 of *Paramārthasāra* :

"*Turīyam grāhya-grāhaka-kṣobha-pralayasaṁskāra-parikṣayāt jñānaghanaprakāśānandamūrti*; *ataḥ tadantaḥsthamapi tābhyo 'vasthābhyaḥ cinmayatayā samuttīrṇatvāt 'paraṁ' anyat-iti*" (p. 80).

126. *Vyāna-śakti*—Macrocosmically it pervades the entire universe and microcosmically it pervades the entire body when the *kuṇḍalinī* becomes awakened, and brings about the *turyātīta* condition.

127. *Turyātīta* means transcending the fourth state. It is a state beyond the *turya*. *Turya* is *turīya* (fourth) in relation to the *three* states of waking, dream and deep sleep; but in *turyātīta*, the above three states as separate states disappear. Hence when the three states have disappeared, *turya* can no longer be called *turya*. It is called *turyātīta* in which the *turya* or fourth state has been transcended. It is a state where pure consciousness is like an ocean without any ruffle whatsoever, and is full of bliss. It is the consciousness of Śiva himself or one who has reached that stage in which the entire universe appears as his Self. In *turya*, *manas* becomes attenuated; in *turyātīta* it is dissolved in *śakti*. When the *turya* state becomes fully developed and reaches perfection, it is transformed into *turyātīta* state. In this state, everything appears to the individual as *Śiva* or Self.

128. *pati*—This refers to the condition in which the individual soul realizes his identity with the universal Self or *pati* or Śiva.

129. In the 9th sūtra, the *saṁsāritva* has been described from the metaphysical point of view; here (in the 12th sūtra), it has been described from the microcosmic point of view both in the individual's *paśu daśā* (bound state) and *pati daśā* (liberated state).

130. It is not clear as to which Pratyabhijñā-ṭīkā is referred to here. Perhaps it may be the untraced *vivṛti* on the Pratyabhijñā-kārikās by Utpalāctārya.

131. *Citta* means the limited individual consciousness, the psychological status of the individual.

132. *Citi* means the universal consciousness, consciousness in its initial, unconditioned state. It is also known as *cit*.

133. *Cetana* in this context means the consciousness of the Self.

134. Utpaladeva or Utpalācārya flourished in about 900-950 A.D. This quotation is from his *Stotrāvalī* in praise of Śiva.

135. The traditional trinity consists of Brahmā, Viṣṇu, and Śiva. Since in this system, Śiva is mostly the term used for the Absolute, Indra has been substituted for Śiva in the trinity.

136. This is a quotation from the *Spandakārikā* (II, 10) of Vasugupta. The full verse is as follows :

तदाक्रम्य बलं मन्त्राः सर्वज्ञबलशालिनः ।
प्रवर्तन्तेऽधिकाराय करणानीव देहिनाम् ॥

i.e. the *mantras* having resorted to that power (of *citi*) alone acquire the power and efficiency of the all-knowing (i.e. Śiva) and then proceed to carry out their specific functions even as the senses of the individual (carry out their specific functions by the power of the individual, not by themselves).

137. *Samāveśa* means *samādhi* in which there is unity-experience, i.e. in which the entire universe appears as Self, in which the consciousness of the empirical Self is completely subordinated, and it becomes identified with the consciousness of Śiva.

138. *Vyutthāna* means literally 'rising up', i.e., rising up from the condition of contemplation to every-day normal experience.

139. *deha-prāṇa-nīla-sukhādiṣu.*

dehaa, prāṇa are examples of the 'subject' in whom *deha* is relatively outer and *prāṇa*, inner; *nīlasukhādiṣu* are examples of 'object' of which again *nīla* is outer experience, and *sukha* is inner experience.

140. *Prāṇa*-śakti here means the primal energy, not prāṇavāyu or the breath of that name. The transformation of consciousness into *prāṇa* is a step towards its progressive materialization. This *prāṇa* is also known as *mahāprāṇa*.

141. '*Madhya* : Madhya-nāḍī,—Madhya from the point of view of Śambhu or Śiva, is the universal consciousness which is the innermost or central reality of all existence, it is the pure I-consciousness of Śiva. From the point of view of Śakti, it is *jñāna-kriyā*—knowledge and action—the spiritual urge which expresses itself in knowledge and action. From the point of view of *aṇu* or the individual, it is the *madhya-nāḍi*.

Madhya-nāḍi : *Madhya or madhyama nāḍi* is the *suṣumnā-nāḍı* which is in between *iḍā* and *piṅgalā nāḍis*. The word *nāḍī* is derived from the root *naḍ* (*bhranś*)—to fall, drop. That through which something drops or flows is *nāḍi*. The *nāḍis* are subtle channels of *prāṇic* energy. *Madhya or madhyamā nāḍi* is so called because it is centrally situated. It is also called *suṣumnā*. The derivation of the word suṣumnā is somewhat uncertain. According to Śabdakalpadruma *'su ṣu' ityaoyaktaśabdam mnāyati* i.e. that which repeats the indistinct sound su ṣu (सुषु√म्ना) may be its derivation.

Suṣumnā is situated in the interior of the cerebro-spinal axis or Merudaṇḍa. It extends from Mūlādhāra to Sahasrāra. Within the 'fiery red' Tāmasika Suṣumnā is the lustrous Rājasika Vajrā or Vajriṇī Nāḍī and within the Vajriṇī is the pale Sāttvika Citrā or Citriṇī. It is the interior of the Citriṇī which is called Brahma-nāḍī. Suṣumnā is said to be fire like (*Vahnisvarūpā*) ; Vajriṇī is said to be sun-like (*sūryasvarūpā*) ; Citriṇi is said to be moon-like (*candrasvarūpā*). The opening at the end of the *Citriṇī nāḍī* is called Brahmadvāra. It is through this that Kuṇḍalinī mounts up.

Iḍā and Piṅgalā *nāḍis* are outside *suṣumnā* and run in a parallel way over it. Iḍā is on the left and Piṅgalā on the right. They are curved like a bow. These three (Iḍā, Piṅgalā and Suṣumnā) join at the Ājñā cakra which is known as Triveṇī or the confluence of the three.

Some have taken *nāḍis* and *cakras* to mean nerve and ganglia. They are not physical constituents. They are constituents of the *prāṇamaya-kośa*, the vital sheath in the *sūkṣma śarira* (the subtle body). Only their impact in the physical body is felt through the nerves and the ganglia. The *cakras* are the seats of *śakti*.

142. *Brahma-randhra*. According to Tantra, there are *cakras* or centres of prāṇa located in the *praṇā-maya-kośa*. These are called *cakras*, because they are like a wheel in appearance. They absorb and distribute *prāṇa* or vitality to the *prāṇamaya-kośa*, and through it to the physical body.

When the higher *cakras* are fully activated, they impart to the individual certain subtle and occult experiences. Their names together with the nearest physical organs are given below :

	Nearest physical organ	Cakras
1.	Spinal Centre of region below the genitals.	Mūlādhāra
2.	Spinal Centre of region above the genitals.	Svādhiṣṭhāna
3.	Spinal Centre of region of the navel.	Maṇipūra
4.	Spinal Centre of region of the heart.	Anāhata
5.	Spinal Centre of region at the base of the throat.	Viśuddha
6.	Between the eye-brows	Ājñā
7.	Top of the head	Sahasrāra or Brahmarandhra

143. *Adho-vaktra* (lit., the lower organ) is the *meḍhra-kanda* which is situated below *mūlādhāra* at the root of the rectum.

144. Palāśa is the *butea frondosa* or the Dhāka tree as it is otherwise called. *Suṣumnā* is compared to the mid-rib of

the *palāśa* leaf, and *nāḍīs* springing from it are compared to to fine veinlets joined to the midrib of the *palāśa*.

145. "When, however, the exalted *samvit*......above." This refers to the development from the Śāmbhavopāya and Śāktopāya points of view.

146. *brahmanādi* is the same as the *madhya-nāḍī* or *suṣumnā*.

147. "When the central *brahmanāḍī* develops." This refers to the development from the *āṇavopāya* point of view.

148. *prāṇāyāma* means breath control. There are various methods of breath control in books on *yoga*.

149. *mudrā*—The word literally means 'seal', 'mark'. In yoga, it means certain positions of fingers practised in yogic discipline. In a wider sense, it also means control of certain organs and senses that help in concentration; also concentration, e.g., Bhairavī-mudrā. See *Gheraṇḍasaṁhitā*, Upadeśa 3.

150. *bandha*—This is a yogic practice in which certain organs of the body are contracted or locked.

151. See note 48.

152. *turya* (lit., fourth) is the same as *turiya*. See note 84. It is the state in which there is pure consciousness of *ātman*, and the sense of difference disappears. In this *Udāna* śakti is active.

153. *turyātita*—This is the state higher than *turya*. Unity consciousness that began in *turya* is consummated in *turyātita* in which the whole universe appears as the Self. See *Īśvarapratyabhijñā-vimarśini*, Vol. II, pp. 246-247. In *turyātita*, *vyāna śakti* is active. See note 127.

154. *Kaṭha Upaniṣad* really belongs to the black Yajurveda. The original reading is '*icchan*' (wishing; seeking); the reading here adopted is *aśnan* (eating, tasting). In this context *aśnan* means 'wishing to taste.'

155. There are two states of clear Self-consciousness, viz; *Śāntodita*, and *nityodita*. In the first, there may be diminution of the clarity of self-consciousness some times, but in the second, Self-consciousness is complete and permanent.

156. *Ūrdhva-Kuṇḍalinī*—This is the condition where the *prāṇa* and *apāna* enter the *suṣumnā* and the *kuṇḍalinī* rises up. Kuṇḍalini is a distinct *śakti* that lies folded up in three

and half *valayas* or folds in Mūlādhāra. When she rises from one-three-fourths of the folds, goes up through *suṣumnā*, crosses Lambikā and pierces Brahmarandhra, she is known as *Ūrdhva-kuṇḍalini*, and this pervasion of hers is known as *vikāsa* or *viṣa*. Lambikā is the *prāṇic* cross-road of four *prāṇic* channels, near the palate. The first two channels are for the flow of *prāṇa* for all the *jīvas*. The third channel is that through which the *yogin* rises from *mūlādhāra* by means of *ūrdhva-kuṇḍalini* to Brahmarandhra, as described here. The fourth channel is for those accomplished *yogins* whose *prāṇavāyu* rises directly to Brahmarandhra without having to pass through *mūlādhāra*.

157. *Adhaḥ-kuṇḍalinī*. Its field is from Lambikā down to one-three-fourths of the folds of *kuṇḍalinī* lying folded in the *mūlādhāra*. Prāṇa goes down in *adhaḥ-kuṇḍalinī* from Lambikā towards *mūlādhāra*. This is known as *saṅkoca* or *vahni*.

158. *Ṣaṣṭha-vaktra*. Prof. Leidecker translates *vaktra* as mouth, and thinks that 'sixth mouth' is unintelligible. *Vaktra* in this context does not mean 'mouth'. It means here simply organ. The ears, eyes, nose, mouth, and the anus are, in this system, known as *pañca-vaktra* or five organs and *meḍhra-kanda* near the root of the rectum, which is below mūlādhāra is the *ṣaṣṭha-vaktra*, the sixth organ.

159. *Vahni-viṣa* : *Vahni* refers to *adhaḥ-kuṇḍalinī* and *viṣa* to *ūrdhva-kuṇḍalinī*. The entrance into the *adhaḥ-kuṇḍalinī* is *saṅkoca* or *vahni*; rising into *ūrdhva-kuṇḍalinī* is *vikāsa* or *viṣa*. *Vahni* is symbolic of *prāṇa vāyu* and *viṣa* of *apāna vāyu*. When *prāṇa* enters the *suṣumnā* and goes down into *adhaḥ-kuṇḍalinī* or *mūlādhāra*, then this condition is known as *vahni*. Entering into the full portion of the root and half of the middle of *adhaḥ-kuṇḍalinī* is known as *vahni* or *saṅkoca*. *Vahni* is derived from the root *'vah'*—to carry. Since *prāṇa* is carried down upto *mūlādhāra* in this state, it is called *vahni*. In Sanskrit, *vahni* means 'fire'. In this sense also, the root meaning of *'vah'*—to carry is implied. Fire is called *vahni*, because it carries the oblations to the *devas* (gods). The *āveśa* or entering into the remaining half of the *madhya* or middle and full portion of the *agra* or tip of the *adhaḥ-kuṇḍalinī* right upto the lowest spot of *ūrdhva-kuṇḍalinī* is known as *viṣa*.

The word *viṣa* does not mean poison here. It is derived from the root '*viṣ*' to pervade. *Viṣa*, therefore, refers to *prasara* or *vikāsa*. Poison is also called *viṣa* because it pervades the whole body.

What is meant to be conveyed is that when the *prāṇa* and *apāna* enter the *suṣumnā*, the *citta* or individual consciousness should be stopped or suspended between the *vahni* and *viṣa* or in other words between the *adhaḥ-kuṇḍalinī* and the *ūrdhva-kuṇḍalinī*.

Vāyupūrṇa—full of *vāyu* means that the *citta* should be restrained in such a way that *vāyu* may neither pass out through the nostrils nor through the male organ and the anus. *Citta* and *vāyu* are inter-connected. Restraint of one brings about the restraint of the other.

160. *Smarānanda* (bliss of sexual union). When the *citta* can be restrained between the *adhaḥ* and *ūrdhva kuṇḍalinī* in this way, then one has the joy of sexual union. This is 'inverted' kāma. Sexual union is external; this union is internal.

161. This refers to the yogic practice of the school. Perfection is accomplished by the development of "*madhya*" which in the case of *aṇu* or the individual *jīva* means the development of *prāṇa-śakti* in the *suṣumnā* which is in the *madhya* or between the *iḍā* and *piṅgalā nāḍis*. One way of the development of *madhya* is the *saṅkoca* and *vikāsa* of the *śakti*. The literal translation of *saṅkoca* and *vikāsa* can hardly do justice to the yogic practice indicated by these. *Saṅkoca* connotes the following discipline. Even while mind is going forth towards external objects by means of the senses, even while the senses are actively functioning in grasping form, colour, sound, smell, etc., attention is *withdrawn* from them and *turned towards* the inner reality which is the source and background of all activity.

Vikāsa means *concentration* on the inner reality even while the sense-organs are quite open, e.g., the practice of the *bhairavī mudrā*.

Saṅkoca implies *withdrawal of attention* from external objects; *vikāsa* implies *concentration of attention on the inner consciousness and not allowing it to go out at all* even when the eyes, ears, etc., are open to their respective objects. It means remaining steady within like a gold pillar, even while the senses are directed towards their objects.

Saṅkoca and *Vikāsa* have to be further developed by the technique of *prasara-viśrānti* at the level of *ūrdhva-kuṇḍalinī*. *Prasara* is, here, practically synonymous with *vikāsa* and *viśrānti* with *saṅkoca*. The yogin develops the *prāṇa-śakti* in the *suṣumnā*, and by restraining it between the eye-brows, he attains to *ūrdhva-kuṇḍalinī* level. Here he practises *prasaraviśrānti*.

This practice of *saṅkoca* and *vikāsa* has to be developed in *adhaḥ-kuṇḍalinī* also. Entering completely into the root and half of the middle of *adhaḥ-kuṇḍalinī* is known as *saṅkoca* or *vahni*, and entering into the remaining half and wholly into the tip of the *adhaḥ-kuṇḍalinī* right up to the position where the *ūrdhva-kuṇḍalinī* ends is known as *vikāsa* or *viṣa* or *unmīlana samādhi*.

162. *anacka* : *aca* = a, i, u, ṛ, ḷ, e, o, ai, au, i.e., all the vowels; 'anacka' is sounding ka, ha, etc. without the vowel. The real meaning of the yogic practice of *anacka* sounding is to concentrate on any *mantra* back to the source where it is unuttered.

163. Leidecker has given a very confused translation of this verse. The following points have to be noted in this verse. This is in praise of *jagadambā*—the world-mother; '*tava*' (your) refers to '*jagadambā*'. '*Anackaka..cchido*'; '*vidhṛta-cetasaḥ*', and '*dāritāndhatamasaḥ*' are compounds qualifying '*hṛdaya-paṅkajasya*'. '*Vidyāṅkuro*' is connected with '*tava*'. Or '*dāritāndha-tamasaḥ*' may be taken, as qualifying '*tava*'.

164. *dvādaśāntaḥ* = a measure of twelve fingers; literally, it means the end of twelve fingers.

165. The *prāṇa* starts at the point of *hṛdaya* (*prāṇollāsa* which here means the centre of the diaphragm and ends (*viśrānti*) at *dvādaśānta*, i.e., at a distance of twelve fingers from the point between the two eye-brows. *Apāna* (vāyu) starts from *dvādaśānta* (distance of twelve fingers), and ceases at *hṛdaya* (centre of the diaphragm). '*Nibhālana*' means fixing the *citta* or mind at the start of *prāṇa* at the heart, and at its cessation at a distance of twelve fingers from the centre of the eye-brows and at the start of *apāna* from *dvādaśānta* and its cessation at *hṛdaya*. This is like the *prāṇāpāna smṛti* (*pāṇāpāna sati*) of Buddhist yoga. This is known as *Śakti-dvādaśānta*, or *kauṇḍalinī*.

There is another *dvādasānta*, over the crown of the head which is known as *Śiva dvādaśānta* or *prakriyānta*.

166. 'Beautiful one' refers to the *devī* (the goddess). This is addressed to the *devi*. Most of the mystic teachings in this system are in the form of a dialogue between Śiva and the Devī (goddess).

167. *unmeṣa* (lit., unfolding) is a technical term of this yoga. Only half of the verse has been quoted in the text. The full verse is as given below:

> *Eka-cintā prasaktasya yataḥ syād aparodayaḥ,*
> *unmeṣaḥ sa tu vijñeyaḥ svayam tam upalakṣayet.*

This means while one is engaged in one thought and another arises, then resting mentally at the junction point between the two is known as *unmeṣa*. One can see that for oneself. The nature of mind is to pass successively from thought to thought, but if one rests mentally immediately after one thought and just before another thought arises, one develops the quality of *unmeṣa*. It means resting in the *spanda* between two thoughts or images, i.e., resting in the consciousness which is the background of both the thoughts or images. It is the unfoldment of the creative nature of the Supreme. This is the explanation according to *Śāktopāya*.

According to *Śāmbhavopāya*, the emergence of the *pāramārthika bhāva* or the highest reality, while one is engaged in meditating on the object of one's devotion is known as *unmeṣa*.

168. Three methods have been recommended here for rising to the highest bliss by concentrating on aesthetic enjoyment, viz., (1) *āsvāda-dhāraṇā*, concentrating on the savour of eating and drinking, (2) *śabda-dharāṇā*, concentrating on the aesthetic enjoyment of music, and (3) *manastuṣṭi-dhāraṇā*, concentrating on whatever pleases the mind.

169. For the meaning of *samāveśa*, see Abhinavagupta :

> आवेशश्चास्वतंत्रस्य स्वतद्रूपनिमज्जनात् ।
> परतद्रूपता शम्भोराद्याच्छक्त्यविभागिनः ॥

—*Tantrāloka* I, 173

Āveśa or Saṃāveśa means mergence of the helpless, limited self into and becoming identical with Supreme Śiva who is at one with the primal Śakti. *Samāveśa* means subordinating one's limited nature, and acquiring the nature of the Supreme.

170. *Vyutthāna*—Literally 'rising'. In yoga, it means coming to normal consciousness after contemplation.

171. *Nimīlana-samādhi* is the inward meditation with closed eyes in which the individual consciousness is absorbed in the universal consciousness. In this even the trace of object as object disappears and it becomes one with *cit.* This is real introversion or *antarmukhatā*, and leads to full I-consciousness or *pūrṇāhantā*.

172. *Krama-mudrā or Mudrā-Krama.* This is defined in the text itself by the Krama-sūtra. In this, the mind swings alternately between the internal and the external. The internal appears as the universal consciousness, and the external no longer appears as merely the world, but as the form of Śiva or universal consciousness. *Mudrā*, here is not used in its ordinary sense of certain postures and positions of fingers, etc. The sense in which it is used here is given further on in the text itself.

173. *samvit-devatā-cakram*—From the macrocosmic point of view, the *samvit-devatās* are the *khecari-cakra, gocari-cakra, dik-cari-cakra*, and *bhūcari-cakra* described earlier. From the microcosmic point of view this consists of limited knowership, internal and external senses, and limited objective knowledge.

174. *Kālāgnyādeḥ carama-kalā-paryantasya*—From Rudra known as kālāgni-bhuvaneśa in Nivṛttikalā i.e. the lowest phase of manifestation upto the highest phase of manifestation known as śāntā-kalā. Kalā here means phase of manifestation. See the chart of manifestation on p. 156.

175. *parā-bhaṭṭārikā* here refers to the highest *vimarśa*. There are three kinds of vimarśa, viz., *para, apara* and *parāpara*.

Para is the *vimarśa* of Śiva in which there is *abheda* or complete non-difference between 'I' and 'this', 'knower' and 'known'; *apara* is the *vimarśa* of *aṇu* or the empirical individual in which there is *bheda* or difference between 'I' and 'this', knower and known; *parāpara* is the *vimarśa* of *śakti* in which there is *bhedābheda* in which the difference between 'I' and 'this' is posited and for ever transcended.

Vide Note No. 174

KALĀS AND BHUVANAS ACCORDING TO ABHINAVAGUPTA

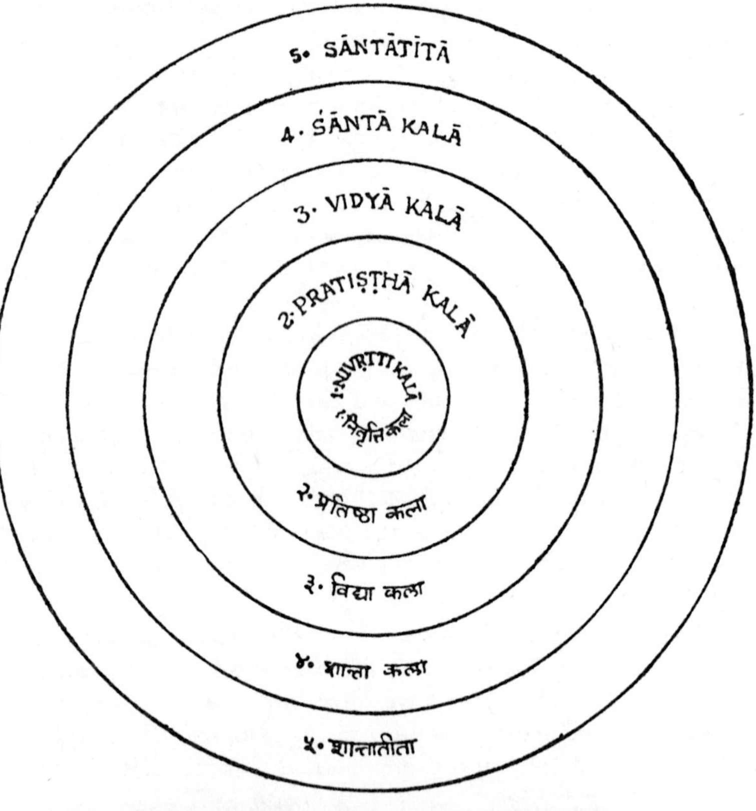

EXPLANATORY NOTE ON THE DIAGRAM

The whole manifestation is divided into five *Kalās* or phases. The lowest is:

1. NIVṚTTI-KALĀ. It is formed mainly of *pṛthvī tattva* and has 16 *bhuvanas* or planes of existence. The lowest plane of *Nivṛtti Kalā* is called *Kālāgni rudra-bhuvana*. It is this *bhuvana* that *Kṣemarāja* refers to in '*Kālāgnyādeḥ*'.

2. PRATIṢṬHĀ KALĀ. This is the second *Kalā* counting from the lowest *Kalā*, viz., *Nivṛtti Kalā*. This consists of 23 *tattvas*, from *jala-tattva* upto *prakṛti tattva*, and contains 56 *bhuvanas*.

3. VIDYĀ KALĀ. This third *Kalā* contains seven *tattvas* from *puruṣa tattva* upto *māyā tattva*, and 28 *bhuvanas*.

4. ŚĀNTĀ KALĀ. This fourth *Kalā* contains three *tattvas*, viz., *Śuddha Vidyā*, *Īśvara* and *Sadāśiva*, and 18 *bhuvanas*.

5. ŚĀNTĀTĪTĀ KALĀ. This fifth *Kalā* is comprised of only *Śiva* and *Śakti tattvas* and has no *bhuvana*.

Parama Śiva transcends all *Kalās*.

The total of *bhuvanas* is 16+56+28+18 i.e. 118.

176. *Camatkāra* is the wonderful joy of creativity. Here it means *aham-vimarśa*—the bliss of *perfect Self-consciousness* i. e. *the bliss of the consciousness of the entire manifestation as I. This aham-vimarśa* is the result of the feeling of one-ness of being with *prakāśa* (consciousness-existence). Regarding *prakāśa* and *vimarśa*, see Note 20. The ultimate is *prakāśa-vimarśa-maya*. It is both the universe in its manifested and unmanifested state, and also its permanent substratum.

177. *Kṣemarāja* gives here the ascending stages of reality. The first is *saṃvedya* or *prameya* i.e. the known. The second is *saṃvedana* or *pramāṇa* i. e. knowledge. The third is the *pramātā* or the experient who has self-consciousness. The fourth and deeper stage of reality is that of Sadāśiva whose consciousness is not identified with the limiting adjuncts of body etc., but whose body is the whole universe. The highest stage of reality is Maheśvara whose consciousness of Self is inclusive of entire manifestation and identical with his *prakāśa*.

178. *Jagadānanda* is a technical word of this system and means the bliss of the Self appearing as the universe. The universe in this system is not a fall from the bliss of the Divine; it is rather the bliss of the Divine made visible. Cf. the following verses of Abhinavagupta :

यत्र कोऽपि व्यवच्छेदो नास्ति यद्विश्वतः स्फुरत् ।
यदनाहतसंवित्ति परमामृतबृंहितम् ॥
यत्रास्ति भावनादीनां न मुख्या कापि संगतिः ।
तदेव जगदानन्दमस्मभ्यं शंभुरूचिवान् ।

—*Tantrāloka*, V. 50-51.

That in which there is no division or limitation, for it flashes forth all round, in which the consciousness is intact, i.e. in which it is consciousness alone which expresses itself whether as knower or means of knowledge or as known, that which increases and expands by the nectar of divine joy of absolute sovereignty in which there is no need for imagination or meditation. Śambhu told me that that was *jagadānanda*. The commentator says :

जगता निजानन्दाद्यात्मना विश्वेन रूपेणानन्दो यत्र यतश्चेति जगदानन्दशब्दवाच्यम् ।

That is *jagadānanda* where the universe appears as a visible form of the bliss of the Self. Śambhu referred to in the above verse was the chief *guru* of Abhinavagupta in Trikasystem.

179. According to Tantra there is a correspondence between the *parā-śakti*, the ultimate divine creative power which brings about the sum total of all objects and the *parāvāk* which is the ultimate divine word, the source of the sum total of words. By means of *mantras* which consist of words or letters, one can establish contact with the various *śaktis*. Every word is a *vācaka* or indicator and every object is *vācya* or the indicated. The *vācya* or object is nothing but the intent of the divine word, the divine word made visible.

The divine words or letters are, however, *a-māyīya* out of the scope of māyā. Words are of two kinds, viz., *māyīya* (pertaining to māyā) and *a-māyīya* (not pretaining to māyā). Māyīya words are those on which the meaning is imposed by convention; they are *vikalpas* or fancied constructions; *a-māyīya* words are those which are *nirvikalpaka*, whose meaning is just the *real*, which do not depend on fancy, imposition, supposition or convention, which are *cinmaya*.

180. *akula*:—"*kulam śaktiriti proktam, akulam Śiva ucyate*" (*Svacchanda tantra*) i.e. *kula* is śakti and *akula* is Śiva. Kula (total) or the entire manifestation is *śakti*. One who is not lost in this total (manifestation) is *akula* i.e. Śiva. The letter 'a' from the point of view of *mātṛkā-cakra* is of the nature of Śiva.

181. *pratyāhāra* here does *not* mean 'withdrawing the *citta* from the elements', as Prof. Leidecker makes out in his note, 227. The word '*pratyāhāra*' has been used here in the technical sense of Sanskrit Grammar which means the 'comprehension of several letters or affixes into one syllable, effected by combining the first letter of a sūtra with its final indicatory letter.' Thus the *pratyāhāra*, '*ac*' means a, i, u, ṛ, ḷ, e, o, for it combines the first letter 'a' and the final indicatory letter 'c' of the following sūtras—अइउण्, ऋऌक्, एओङ्, ऐऔच्.

So here the pratyāhāra of 'a' the first letter, and 'ha' the final letter would be 'aha', which suggests 'aham', meaning 'I' or Self. 'Aha' includes all the letters of the Sanskrit language, and since each letter is indicative of an object, 'aha' suggests the sum-total of all objects, viz., the universe. The entire universe lies in the highest Reality or Maheśvara in an undifferentiated state.

182. *bindu* : This means a drop, a dot. In the definite calm of the Highest Reality (anuttara), there arises a metaphysical Point of stress. This is known as *bindu.* In this, the universe to be, lies gathered up into a point. This bindu is known as *ghanībhūtā śakti*—the creative forces compacted into a Point. It is as yet undifferentiated into objects. It is the *cidghana* or massive consciousness in which lie potentially in an undifferentiated mass all the worlds and beings to be manifested. Therefore, the text says that 'a' and 'ha' joined into 'aha', and thus *together* summing up the entire manifestation lie undifferentiated into a Point in the Highest Reality. A point is indicative of non-differentiation. From the point of view of language, the 'bindu' in Sanskrit is indicated by *anusvāra*—the nasal sound marked by a dot on a letter. Bindu is thus the *anusvāra*, and this completes 'aha' into 'aham' (अहं). This *anusvāra*, after having joined, 'a' and 'ha' in oneness shows that all manifestation though appearing emanated and different is actually residing in Śiva, and is not different ftom him. 'A' respresents Śiva; 'ha' represents Śakti; the anusvāra represents the fact that though Śiva is manifested right upto the earth through Śakti, he is not divided thereby; he remains undivided (*avibhāga-vedanātmaka-bindu-rūpatayā*).

183. '*mahāhrada*'—the great or deep lake refers to the Supreme Spiritual awareness. It has been called a great or deep lake, because it is clear, uncovered by anything, infinite and deep.

184. *Cakravarti* has a double sense here—(1) ruler of the cakra i.e. circle or group of sense-deities and (2) universal sovereign.

185. When the senses are divinised, they become *saṁvit-devatā-cakra* i.e., *karaṇeśvarīs*.

GLOSSARY OF TECHNICAL TERMS

A—symbol of *Śiva*.

ĀBHĀSANA—appearance; esoteric meaning—*sṛṣṭi* — emanation.

ADHAḤ-KUṆḌALINĪ—the field of *Kuṇḍalinī* from *Lambikā* to one-three-fourths of its folds in the *Mūlādhāra* (see note No. 157.)

ADHO-VAKTRA—*Meḍhra-Kanda,* situated at the root of the rectum.

ĀDIKOṬI—the first edge or point; i.e.—, the heart from which the measure of breath is determined.

AHAṀ-BHĀVA—I-feeling; I-consciousness.

AHANTĀ—'I'-consciousness; I-ness.

AKHYĀTI—ignorance.

AKULA—*Śiva.*

ALAṀGRĀSA—bringing experienced object completely to sameness with the consciousness of the Self, when no impression of saṁsāra as separate from consciousness is allowed to remain.

AMĀYĪYA—beyond the scope of *Māyā*; *Amāyīya Śabdas* are the words whose meaning does not depend on convention or supposition, where the word and the object are one.

ANACKA—lit., sounding the consonants without the vowels; esoteric meaning—'concentrating on any *mantra* back to the source where it is unuttered'.

ĀNANDA—bliss, the nature of *Śakti.*

ANANTABHAṬṬĀRAKA—the presiding deity of the *Mantra* experients.

ANĀŚRITA-ŚIVA—the state of Śiva in which there is no objective content yet, in which the universe is negated from Him.

ĀṆAVA MALA—*mala* pertaining to *aṇu* i.e., innate ignorance of the *jiva*; primary limiting condition which reduces universal consciousness to a *jiva* depriving, consciousness of Śakti and Śakti of consciousness and thus bringing about sense of imperfection.

ANTAKOṬI—the last edge or point; it is *dvādaśānta*—a measure of twelve fingers.

ANTARMUKHĪBHĀVA—introversion of consciousness.

ANUGRAHA—grace.

ANUTTARA—the Highest, the Supreme, the Absolute (lit., one than whom nothing is higher).

APĀNA—the vital *vāyu* that goes in downwards towards the anus.

APARA—lower or lowest.

APAVARGA—liberation.

ĀRHATA—Jaina.

ARTHA—object; end; sense-object; meaning; notion; aim.

ASAT—non-being.

ĀŚYĀNATĀ—shrunken state; dried state; congealment; solidification.

ĀTMASĀTKṚ—assimilate to the Self.

ĀTMA-VIŚRĀNTI—resting in the Self.

AVYAKTA—unmanifest.

BAHIRMUKHATĀ—extroversion of consciousness.

BAHIRMUKHĪBHĀVA—externalization; extroversion.

BAINDAVĪ KALĀ—*Baindavī*—pertaining to *Bindu* or the Knower, *Kalā*—will-power. *Baindavī Kalā* is that freedom of Parama Śiva by which the knower always remains the knower and is never reduced to the known.

BALA—*Cid-bala*, power of the true Self or Universal Consciousness.

BANDHA—bondage; yogic practice in which certain organs of the body are contracted and locked.

BHAIRAVA—*Parama Śiva*; the Highest Reality. This is an anacrostic word, '*bha*' indicating '*bharaṇa*' maintenance of the world, '*ra*', '*ravaṇa*' or withdrawal of the world, and '*va*' '*vamana*', or projection of the world.

BHĀVA—existence—both internal and external; object.

BHOGA—experience, sometimes used in the narrow sense of 'enjoyment'.

BHOKTĀ—experient.

BHŪCARĪ—sub-species of *Vāmeśvarī*, connected with the *bhāvas* or existent objects. *Bhū* means existence; hence existent objects are the sphere of '*bhūcarī*'.

BHŪMIKĀ—role.

BHUVANA—becoming; place of existence; world; place of being, abode.

BĪJĀVASTHĀPANA—setting of the seed, esoteric meaning, '*vilaya*' —concealment of true nature.

BINDU—written also as Vindu, a point; a metaphysical point; *ghanībhutā śakti*,—the compact mass of *Śakti* gathered into an undifferentiated point ready to create; also *paraḥ pramātā*—the highest Self or Consciousness; the *anusvāra* or nasal sound indicated by a dot on a letter indicating the fact that *Śiva* in spite of the manifestation of the universe is undivided. (See Note 182).

BRAHMANĀḌĪ—*suṣumnā* or the central *prāṇic nāḍi*.

BRAHMARANDHRA—the *Sahasrāra Cakra*.

BRAHMAVĀDA—in this system—*Śāṅkara Vedānta*.

BUDDHI—Sometimes the higher mind; the super-personal mind; the ascertaining intelligence, intuitive aspect of consciousness by which the essential Self awakens to truth.

CAMATKĀRA—bliss of the pure I-consciousness; delight of artistic experience.

CARAMAKALĀ—the highest phase of manifestation known as Śāntyatīta or Śāntātītākalā.

CĀRVĀKA—the materialist.

CĀRVĀKA DARŚANA—materialistic philosophy.

CETANA—self; *Paramaśiva*; soul, conscious individual.

CETYA—knowable; object of consciousness.

CHEDA—cessation of *prāṇa* and *apāna* by the sounding of *anacka* sounds.

CIDĀNANDA—lit., consciousness and bliss, the nature of ultimate reality; the bliss of universal consciouness.

CINTĀ—thought; idea.

CIT—the Absolute; foundational consciousness; the unchanging principle of all changes.

CITI—the consciousness—power of the Absolute that brings about the world-process.

CITI-CAKRA— *Saṁvit-Cakra*:—the senses.

CITTA—the individual mind, the limitation of Citi or Universal Consciousness manifested in the individual mind, consisting mainly of Sattva, the mind of the Māyā-pramātā.

DARŚANA—seeing; system of philosophy.

DEŚA—space.

DIKCARĪ—sub-species of *Vāmeśvarī*, connected with the *Bahiṣkaraṇa* or outer senses. *Dik* means 'space'. Outer senses have to do with space; hence they are the sphere of '*dikcarī*'.

GOCARĪ—sub-species of *Vāmeśvarī*, connected with the *antaḥkaraṇa* of the experient. '*Go*' means 'sense'; *antaḥkaraṇa* is the seat of the senses; hence *Gocarī* is connected with *antaḥkaraṇa*.

GRĀHAKA—knower; subject.

GRĀHYA—known; object.

HA—symbol of *Śakti*.

HAṬHAPĀKA—persistent process of assimilating experience to the consciousness of the experient.

HETU—cause.

HETUMAT—effect.

HṚDAYA—heart; central consciousness (in *Yoga*).

ICCHĀ—Will, the *Śakti* of *Sadāśiva*.

IDANTĀ—'This'-consciousness.

ĪŚVARA-TATTVA—the 4th *tattva* of the system, counting from *Śiva*. In this the consciousness of 'I' and 'This' is equally prominent. The consciousness of *Sadā-Śiva* is 'I am this'. The consciousness of *Īśvara* is 'This am I.' *Jñāna* is predominant in this *tattva*.

ĪŚVARABHAṬṬĀRAKA—the presiding deity of the Mantreśvaras residing in *Īśvaratattva*.

JAGADĀNANDA—the bliss of the Self or the Divine appearing as the universe; the bliss of the Divine made visible. (See Note 178).

JAGAT—the world process.
JĀGRAT—the waking condition.
JĪVA—the individual; the individual soul; the empirical self.
JĪVANMUKTI—liberation while one is alive.
JÑĀNA—knowledge, the *Śakti* of *Īśvara.*

KALĀ—limited agency; creativity; phase of manifestation; part letter or word (in *ha-kalāparyantam*).
KĀLA—time; *Śakti* or power that determines succession.
KĀLĀGNI—the lowest *bhuvana* or plane of existence in *Nivṛtti Kalā.* (See Note 174).
KAÑCUKA—covering.
KĀRAṆA—cause
KARAṆEŚVARYAḤ—Khecarī, Gocarī, Dikcarī and Bhūcarī cakra.
KĀRMAMALA—*mala* due to *vāsanas* or impressions left behind on the mind due to *karma* or action.
KĀRYA—effect.
KHECARĪ—sub-species of *Vāmeśvari Śakti*, connected with the *pramātā*, the empirical self. *Khecari* is one that moves in '*kha*' or '*ākāśa*', symbol of consciousness.
KHYĀTI—jñāna; knowledge; wisdom.
KRIYĀ—action, the *Śakti* of *Śuddha-vidyā.*
KULA—*Śakti.*
KULĀMNĀYA—the Śākta system or doctrine.

MADHYA—the Central Consciousness—*Saṁvit*; the pure I-consciousness; the *Suṣumnā* or central *prāṇic nāḍi.*
MADHYADHĀMA—*Suṣumnā*, the central-*nāḍi* in the *prāṇamaya-kośa*, also known as *brahmanāḍi.*
MADHYAMĀ—*Śabda* in its subtle form as existing in the mind or *antaḥkaraṇa* prior to its gross manifestation.
MADHYAŚAKTI—*Saṁvit-Śakti*, the Central Consciousness-power.
MĀDHYAMIKA—follower of the *madhyamaka* system of Buddhist philosophy.
MAHĀMANTRA—the great *mantra* i.e., of pure consciousness.
MAHĀRTHA—the greatest end; the highest value; the pure I-consciousness; the krama discipline.

MAHEŚVARA—the highest lord, *Parama-Śiva*—the Absolute.

MĀHEŚVARYA—the power of *Maheśvara*.

MALA—dross; ignorance which hampers the free expression of the spirit.

MANTREŚVARA—the experient who has realized *Īśvara tattva*.

MANTRA—the experient who has realized the *Śuddha vidyā-tattva*; sacred words or formula to be reflected on and chanted.

MANTRA-MAHEŚVARA—the experient who has realized *Sadā-Śiva tattva*.

MĀYĀ—from '*mā*' to measure, the finitising or limiting principle of the Divine; a *tattva* below *Śuddha vidyā*, the principle of veiling the Infinite and projecting the finite; the source of the five *kañcukas*; the finitising power of *Parama Śiva*.

MĀYĀPRAMĀTĀ—the empirical self,governed by *Māyā*.

MĀYĪYA MALA—*mala* due to *Māyā* which gives to the soul its gross and subtle body, and brings about sense of difference.

MEYA (PRAMEYA)—object.

MĪMĀṀSAKA—the follower of the *Mimāṁsā* system of philosophy.

MOKṢA—liberation.

MUDRĀ—*mud* (joy) *ra* (to give). It is called *mudrā*, because it gives the bliss of spiritual consciousness or because it seals up (*mudraṇāt*) the universe into the being of the *turīya* consciousness; also, yogic control of certain organs as help in concentration.

MUDRĀ-KRAMA or KRAMAMUDRĀ--the condition in which the mind by the force of *samāveśa* swings alternately between the internal (Self or Śiva) and the external (the world which now appears as the form of Śiva).

MUKTI—liberation.

NAIYĀYIKA—the follower of Nyāya philosophy; logician; dialectician.

NIBHĀLANA—perception; mental practice.

NIMEṢA—lit., closing of the eye; dissolution of the world.

NIMĪLANA-SAMĀDHI—the inward meditative condition in which the individual consciousness gets absorbed into the Universal Consciousness.

NITYATVA—eternity.

NIYATI—limitation by cause-effect relation; spatial limitation.

PANCAKṚTYA—the five-fold act of *sṛṣṭi*, *sthiti*, *saṁhāra*, *vilaya* and *anugraha* or the five-fold act of ābhāsana, rakti, vimarśana, bījāvasthāpana, vilāpana.

PĀÑCARĀTRA—the philosophy of Vaiṣṇavism, the follower of such philosophy.

PĀÑCARĀTRIKA—followers of *Pāñcarātra* system.

PARA—highest.

PARĀMARŚA—seizing mentally; experience; comprehension; remembrance.

PARAMA ŚIVA—the Highest Reality; the Absolute.

PARĀPARA—intermediate stage; both identical and different; unity in diversity.

PARA-PRAMĀTĀ—the highest Experient; *Parama-Śiva.*

PARĀ-ŚAKTI—highest *Śakti* of the Divine; *Citi.*

PARĀVĀK—the unmanifest *Śakti* or vibratory movement of the Divine; Logos; cosmic ideation.

PARICCHINNA—limited.

PARIṆĀMA—transformation.

PARAMĀRTHA—highest reality; essential truth; the highest goal.

PĀŚA—bondage.

PAŚU—one who is bound; the individual soul.

PAŚYANTĪ—the divine view of the universe in undifferentiated form; *Vāk Śakti* going forth as 'seeing', manifesting, ready to create in which there is no differentiation between *vācya* (object) and *vācaka* (word).

PATI—lord; *Śiva.*

PATIDAŚĀ—the status of the highest experient; the state of liberation.

PRAKĀŚA—lit., light; the principle of Self-revelation; consciousness; the principle by which every thing else is known.

PRAKṚTI—the source of objectivity from Buddhi down to earth.

PRALAYĀKALA or PRALAYAKEVALIN—resting in *māyā tattva*, not cognisant of anything.

PRAMĀṆA—means of knowing; proof.

PRAMĀTĀ—the knower, the subject, the experient.

PRAMEYA—object of knowledge; known; object.

PRĀṆA—generic name for the vital *Śakti*: specifically it is the vital *vāyu* in expiration; vital energy; life energy.

PRĀṆĀYĀMA—breath-control.

PRASARA—lit., expansion, manifestation of *Śiva* in the form of the universe through His *Śakti*.

PRATH—to expand; unfold; appear; shine.

PRATHĀ—the mode of appearance; the way.

PRATYABHIJÑĀ—re-cognition.

PRATYĀHĀRA—comprehension of several letters or affixes into one syllable effected by combining the first letter of a sūtra with its final indicatory letter. (see Note 181). In yoga, withdrawal of the senses from their objects.

PRITHIVĪ—the earth *tattva*.

PŪRṆĀHANTĀ—the perfect I-consciousness, non-relational I-consciousness.

PŪRṆATVA—perfection.

PURYAṢṬAKA—lit., 'the city of the group of eight'—i.e., the five *tanmātras, buddhi, ahaṁkāra and manas*'; the *sūkṣmaśarīra* consisting of the above eight constituents.

RĀGA—One of the kañcukas of Māyā on account of which there is limitation by desire.

RAJAS—the principle of motion, activity and disharmony—a constituent of *Prakṛti*.

RAKTI—relish; enjoyment esoteric meaning—'sthiti'—maintenance.

ŚABDA—word.

ŚABDA-BRAHMA—Ultimate reality in the form of vibration of which human word is a gross representation. In this state thought and word are one. (See Notes 74-75).

SADĀŚIVA—the third *tattva*, counting from *Śiva*. At this stage the I-experience is more prominent than the 'this'-experience. This *tattva* is also known as *Sādākhya* inasmuch as '*sat*' or being is posited at this stage. *Icchā* or Will is predominant in this *tattva*.

SAHAJA—natural (from the point of view of the Universal Consciousness).

SAKALA—All the *jīvas* from gods down to the mineral who rest in *māyā tattva.* They have no knowledge of the real self and their consciousness is only that of diversity.

ŚAKTI-PĀTA—descent of the divine *Śakti*; grace.

ŚAKTI-PRASARA—*Śakti-vikāsa*; emergence from *Samādhi* and retaining that experience.

ŚAKTI-SAṄKOCA—withdrawal of attention from sense-activity and turning it towards the inner reality. (See Note 161).

ŚAKTI-VIKĀSA—concentration of attention on the inner consciousness even when the senses are open to their respective objects. (See Note 155).

ŚAKTI-VIŚRĀNTI—Merging back into *Samādhi* and resting in that condition.

SAMĀDHI—collectedness of mind; mental absorption.

SAMĀNA—the vital *Vāyu* that helps in assimilation of food etc. and brings about equilibrium between *prāṇa* and *apāna.*

SAMĀPATTI—Sometimes synonym of *Samādhi,* consummation, attainment of psychic at-one-ment.

SAMARASA—one having the same feeling or consciousness.

SĀMARASYA—identity of consciousness; unison of *Śiva* and *Śakti.*

SAMĀVEŚA—being possessed by the divine; absorption of the individual consciousness in the divine.

SAṀHĀRA—withdrawal; re-absorption.

SAṀSĀRA—transmigratory existence; world process.

SAṀSĀRIN—a transmigratory being.

SAṀSṚTI—transmigratory existence; the world process.

SAṀVIT—consciousness: supreme consciousness.

SAṀVIT-DEVATĀ—from the macrocosmic point of view; *samvit-devatās* are *khecarī, gocarī, dikcarī* and *bhūcarī.* From the microcosmic point of view this consists of the internal and external senses.

SĀṄKHYA—the system of philosophy that believes in two fundamental realities, viz., *Puruṣa* and *Prakṛti*; the follower of such system.

SAṄKOCA—contraction; limitation.

SARVAJÑATVA—omniscience.

SARVAKARTṚTVA—omnipotence.

ŚĀSANA—*Śastra*; philosophical text.

ṢAṢṬHA-VAKTRA—lit. the sixth organ; *meḍhra-kanda*, near the root of the rectum.

SAT—existence which is consciousness.

SATTVA—the principle of being, light and harmony—a constituent of Prakṛti.

SAUGATA—follower of Buddha.

ŚIVA—the name of the divine in general; good.

ŚIVA-TATTVA—the first of the thirty-six *tattvas*. Main characteristic 'cit'.

SṚṢṬI—letting go; emanation; manifestation.

STHITI—maintenance.

ŚUDDHA-VIDYĀ—(sometimes written briefly as *Vidyā*)—the 5th *tattva* counting from *Śiva*. In this *tattva*, the consciousness of both 'I' and 'This' is equally prominent. Though the universe is seen differently, yet identity runs through it as a thread. There is identity in diversity at this stage. *Kriyā* is predominant in this *tattva*. The consciousness of this stage is 'I am I and also this'.

ŚUDDHĀDHVĀ—the pure path; extra-mundane existence; manifestation of the first five *tattvas* viz., *Śiva, Śakti, Sadāśiva, Īśvara* and *Śuddha-vidyā*.

ŚŪNYA—void; the state in which no object is experienced.

ŚŪNYA-PRAMĀTĀ—having the experience of only void; *pralayākala*.

SUṢUPTI—the condition of dreamless sleep.

SVAPNA—the dream condition.

SVARŪPĀPATTI—attaining to one's real nature or true Self.

SVATANTRA—of absolute will; of unimpeded will.

SVĀTANTRYA—the absolute Will of the Supreme.

SVĀTMASĀTKṚ—to assimilate to oneself; to integrate to oneself.

SVECCHĀ—*Śiva's* or *Śakti's* own will, synonymous with *svātantrya*.

SVARŪPA—one's own form; real nature; essence.

TAMAS—the principle of inertia, and delusion—a constituent of *Prakṛti*.

TĀNTRIKA—follower of *Tantra*; pertaining to Tantra.

TANUTĀ—becoming gradually less; reduction; a state of subtleness.

TARKA-ŚĀSTRA—logic and dialectics.

TATTVA—thatness; the very being of a thing; principle.

TRIKA—the system or philosophy of the triad—(1) *Śiva*, (2) *Śakti*, and (3) *Nara*—the bound soul. Or (1) *para*—the highest, having to do with identity; (2) *parāpara*—identity in difference, and (3) *apara*—difference and sense of difference.

TURĪYA—the fourth state of consciousness beyond the state of waking, dreaming and deep sleep, and stringing together all the states; integral awareness; the Metaphysical Self distinct from the psychological or empirical self; the Sākṣī or witnessing Consciousness.

TURYA—lit., the fourth, same as above.

TURYĀTĪTA—the state of consciousness transcending the *Turīya* state, the state in which the distinctions of the three viz., waking, dreaming and deep sleep states are annulled; that pure blissful consciousness in which there is no sense of difference, in which the entire universe appears as the Self.

UDĀNA—the vital *Vāyu* that goes upward; the Śakti that moves up in Suṣumnā at spiritual awakening.

UDVAMANTĪ—lit., vomiting; externalizing; manifesting.

UNMEṢA—lit., opening of the eye—the start of the world process; in *Śaiva yoga*—unfolding of the spiritual consciousness which comes about by concentrating on the inner consciousness which is the background of ideations or rise of ideas.

UNMĪLANA—unfolding; manifestation.

UNMĪLANA SAMĀDHI—that state of the mind in which, even when the eyes are open, the external world appears as Universal Consciousness or Śiva.

UPĀDĀNA—material cause.

UPĀDHI—limiting adjunct or condition.

ŪRDHVA-KUṆḌALINĪ—the risen up *kuṇḍalinī* when the *prāṇa* and *apāna* enter the *Suṣumnā*.

VĀCAKA—word or indicator.

VĀCYA—object or the indicated, referent.

VĀHA—the *prāṇa* flowing in the *iḍā nāḍi* on the left and *apāna* flowing in the *piṅgalā nāḍi* on the right are together known as *Vāha* (lit., flow).

VAHNI—a technical word of Śaiva-Yoga, meaning 'entering completely' into the root and half of the middle of *adhaḥ kuṇḍalinī*. (from the root *Vah* to carry).

VAIKHARĪ—*Śakti* as gross physical word.

VAIṢṆAVA—the follower of *Viṣṇu*; follower of *Vaiṣṇava* philosophy.

VĀMEŚVARĪ—the divine *Śakti* that emits ('*vam*' to 'emit') or sends forth the universe out of the Absolute, and produces the reverse (*vāma*) consciousness of difference (whereas there is non-difference in the divine).

VIBHŪTI—splendour; power.

VIDYĀ—limited knowledge.

VIGRAHA—individual form or shape; body.

VIGRAHĪ—the embodied.

VYĀNA—the vital *Vāyu* that is everywhere or the pervasive prāṇa.

VIJÑĀNĀKALA—the experient below *Śuddha Vidyā* but above *Māyā*; has pure awareness but no agency. He is free of *kārma* and *māyiyamala* but not yet free of *āṇavamala*.

VIKALPA—difference of perception; diversity; distinction; option; an idea as different from other idea; ideation; fancy; imagination.

VIKALPA-KṢAYA—the dissolution of all *vikalpas*.

VIKALPANAM—the differentiation making activity of the mind.

VIKĀSA—unfoldment, development.

VILĀPANA—dissolution; esoteric meaning—*anugraha*—grace.

VILAYA—concealment.

VIMARŚA—lit., experience; technically—the Self-consciousness of the Supreme, full of *jñāna* and *kriyā* which brings about the world-process.

VIMARŚANA—intuitive awareness: esoteric meaning—*saṁhāra*-absorption.

VIṢA—a technical word of Śaiva Yoga, meaning 'entering into the remaining half and wholly into the top of *adhaḥ-kuṇḍalinī* right upto the position where *ūrdhva-kuṇḍalinī* ends (from the root viṣ, to pervade).

VIŚVA—the universe; the all.

VIŚVAMAYA } immanent.
VIŚVĀTMAKA }

VIŚVOTTĪRṆA—transcendent.

VYĀMOHITATĀ—delusion.

VYĀPAKATVA—all-pervasiveness.

VYUTTHĀNA—lit., 'rising'., coming to normal consciousness after contemplation.

SANSKRIT INDEX

ENGLISH INDEX